FAMILY ISSUES IN THE 21ST CENTURY SERIES

MARRIAGE AND INCARCERATION

FAMILY ISSUES IN THE 21ST CENTURY SERIES

Handbook of Parenting: Styles, Stresses and Strategies
Pacey H. Krause and Tahlia M. Dailey (Editors)
ISBN: 978-1-60741-766-8

Marriage and Incarceration
Leana H. Venten (Editor)
2009 ISBN: 978-1-60692-938-4

FAMILY ISSUES IN THE 21ST CENTURY SERIES

MARRIAGE AND INCARCERATION

LEANA H. VENTEN
EDITOR

Nova Science Publishers, Inc.
New York

For permission to use material from this book please contact us:
Telephone 631-231-7269; Fax 631-231-8175
Web Site: http://www.novapublishers.com

LIBRARY OF CONGRESS CATALOGING-IN-PUBLICATION DATA

Marriage and incarceration / [edited by] Leana H. Venten.
p. cm.
Includes bibliographical references and index.
ISBN 978-1-60692-938-4 (softcover)
1. Married people--Congresses. 2. Imprisonment--Congresses. 3. Parent and child--Congresses. 4. Family violence--Congresses. 5. Marriage counseling--Congresses. I. Venten, Leana H.
HQ519.M36 2009
365'.661--dc22 2009027734

Published by Nova Science Publishers, Inc. ✝ New York

CONTENTS

PREFACE

This book is an overview of the Healthy Marriage Initiative. The purpose of this book is also to understand more fully the strategies for improving outcomes for couples who want to develop healthy marriages during and after one partner's incarceration. By convening a diverse group of experts with research and practice knowledge about incarceration and reentry, marriage strengthening, family processes, and domestic violence, this book will begin to identify research and program development needs that could be addressed by public- and/or private-sector investment in research and practice. Based on facilitated discussion on a variety of topics, the symposium participants will develop a framework for next steps in expanding marriage strengthening education services and research for couples separated by incarceration.

Chapter 1 – In 1996, at a time when the U.S. welfare system began undergoing significant reform, Congress proclaimed that any social welfare system must recognize that marriage is the foundation for a successful society and an essential institution promoting the interests of children. Thus, in its legislative overhaul of the Temporary Assistance to Needy Families (TANF) program, Congress mandated that three out of four of the purposes of the new TANF system would include either direct or indirect promotion of healthy marriage.

Chapter 2 - Experts were invited to provide context on the current prison environment, marriage education, domestic violence, and other issues relevant to the symposium. The purpose of these framing remarks was to stimulate discussion; the participants were not asked to come to a consensus on the most appropriate way to handle these issues, rather the issues were put "on the table" to inform the discussion.

This section reflects the lively presentations and discussion of the issues undertaken by the participants. The symposium organizers structured the agenda (see Appendix A) to focus on research and programming aimed at incarcerated men. While they acknowledged the myriad issues that also relate to female and juvenile offenders, it was thought that due to time constraints and because proposed solutions might be population- specific, it would be more appropriate to target one subgroup rather than the incarcerated population as a whole. Thus, the issues covered below speak specifically to the context of prison interventions for men, the largest group within the offender population.

Chapter 3 - The relative newness of programs aimed at strengthening marriages and families affected by incarceration means that, to date, there has been little comprehensive evaluation of these programs and their long-term effects on reducing recidivism. Nevertheless, the participants at the symposium shared preliminary evidence from the field that does point to early successes in certain areas that may be worthy of replication and further study across different populations and environments. Marriage education for this population can be informed by other marriage education efforts directed at low-income and minority populations, as well as by other family strengthening programs targeted at populations under criminal justice supervision or at risk of incarceration. It should be noted that there was no consensus among the participants on which practices were most effective, and many of these examples were countered with the caveat that all need to be studied in greater depth.

Chapter 4 and 5- While the purpose of this symposium was not to come to consensus on any of the discussion points, nevertheless there were several areas in which the participants indicated a strong degree of momentum is needed to move forward and learn more about marriage-strengthening and responsible fatherhood programs, their long-term successes, and how these can be applied to the incarcerated population. This section summarizes these discussion points.

"To encourage marriage and promote the well-being of children, I have proposed a healthy marriage initiative to help couples develop the skills and knowledge to form and sustain healthy marriages. Research has shown that, on average, children raised in households headed by married parents fare better than children who grow up in other family structures. Through education and counseling programs, faith-based, community, and government organizations promote healthy marriages and a better quality of life for children. By supporting responsible child rearing and strong families, my Administration is seeking to ensure that every child can grow up in a safe and loving home." –President George W. Bush, 2003

"This year, some 600,000 inmates will be released from prison back into society. We know from long experience that if they can't find work or a home or help, they are much more likely to commit crime and return to

prison. So tonight, I propose a 4-year,$300 million prisoner reentry initiative to expand job training and placement services; to provide transitional housing; and to help newly released prisoners get mentoring, including from faith-based groups. America is the land of second chance, and when the gates of the prison

In: Marriage and Incarceration
Editors: Leana H. Venten

ISBN: 978-1-60692-938-4

Chapter 1

INTRODUCTION

Brandy Bauer, Jamie Hart, Anne Hopewell and Naomi Tein
U.S. Department of Health and Human Services
Office of the Assistant Secretary for Planning and Evaluation

A. THE ORIGINS OF THE HEALTHY MARRIAGE INITIATIVE

In 1996, at a time when the U.S. welfare system began undergoing significant reform, Congress proclaimed that any social welfare system must recognize that marriage is the foundation for a successful society and an essential institution promoting the interests of children. Thus, in its legislative overhaul of the Temporary Assistance to Needy Families (TANF) program, Congress mandated that three out of four of the purposes of the new TANF system would include either direct or indirect promotion of healthy marriage.

Promotion of healthy marriage has not been limited to the TANF program – throughout his administration President George W. Bush has reiterated the centrality of marriage and positive parenting to a healthy society. Drawing on evidence that healthy marriages increase longevity, promote better mental and physical health, and increase reported levels of happiness, the President proposed an initiative to help couples that have chosen or are choosing marriage to gain access to services where they can acquire the skills and knowledge necessary to form and sustain healthy marriages.

With these goals in mind, in 2002 the Administration for Children and Families (ACF) within the U.S. Department of Health and Human Services (DHHS) designed the Healthy Marriage Initiative. The Healthy Marriage Initiative promotes marriage in appropriate Federal programs and supports the conduct of demonstration projects in partnership with States and localities, as well as research into marriage and marriage programming. At its core, the Initiative awards a series of Federal grants to States and communities to test new ways to promote and support healthy married-parent families and to encourage responsible fatherhood. The ACF Healthy Marriage Initiative is not about coercing marriage, stigmatizing or legally limiting divorce, keeping people trapped in violent or unhealthy relationships, or withdrawing support from single-parent households. Rather, the Healthy Marriage Initiative is about supporting couples who have a desire to have a healthy marriage in obtaining the skills and knowledge necessary for them to be able to achieve that goal.

The Deficit Reduction Act of 2005 provided additional funding for the ACF Healthy Marriage Initiative by appropriating $150 million annually for healthy marriage promotion and responsible fatherhood initiatives. As the Initiative evolves, more focus is being placed on strengthening marriage and family support among special populations, including African-Americans, Hispanics, and Native Americans.

B. Incarceration Initiatives

Concurrent with initiatives to strengthen marriage and family life, President Bush has emphasized his commitment to give individuals a second chance for success when they are released from prison. Under the President's leadership, the Federal Government has sought to improve outcomes for the roughly 600,000 offenders released from prisons and jails each year. With approximately two-thirds of released offenders facing reincarceration within 3 years of release, recidivism poses serious challenges for the criminal justice system and communities.

In 2003, the Federal Departments of Justice, Labor, Housing and Urban Development, and Health and Human Services established the Serious and Violent Offender Re-entry Initiative (SVORI). SVORI, to date, has provided more than $100 million to State and local grantees to develop community programs, training, and reentry strategies that reduce recidivism and promote healthy outcomes for ex-offenders. The SVORI program takes into account that States and communities are unique and in the best position to determine which elements of reentry initiatives best suit their populations and resources. Therefore, the dozens of SVORI-funded programs are quite diverse, tailoring services to different populations and their service needs. All programs, however, are asked to initiate a three-phase continuum of services that begin in prison and carry on after release into supervision and post-supervision phases. Initial findings from preliminary evaluations of some of the SVORI programs are expected early in 2007.

Subsequent to the establishment of SVORI, in 2004 President Bush proposed a $300 million Prison Re-entry Initiative (PRI) for ex-offenders that would expand job training and placement services, provide transitional housing, and help these individuals find community mentors. In particular, this initiative attempts to harness the experience and resources of faith-based and community groups to help deliver these services. The PRI program expands upon a previous project, Ready4Work, which is bringing together business, faith, criminal justice and community groups partnering to assist offenders with the transition from prison to community and home. The Department of Labor (DOL) has funded 30 community- and faith-based grantees to undertake this work. These efforts are being coordinated with separate funding from the Department of Justice (DOJ) and in coordination with Department of Housing and Urban Development programs and substance abuse treatment programs funded by the Substance Abuse and Mental Health Services Administration (SAMHSA) within the DHHS.

The Department of Justice has funded several other initiatives that focus particularly on the social networks and family issues that many incarcerated and formerly incarcerated face. One such initiative is the Safe Return Initiative, funded by the Violence Against Women Office in the Bureau of Justice Assistance of the DOJ. This initiative is aimed at preventing domestic violence in families where one individual is returning from prison. This initiative is discussed in more detail later in this report. Another DOJ-funded project is Family Justice, a community-based organization in New York that is developing and evaluating innovative methods for working with whole families upon a prisoner's return to the community, including during the probation phase.

C. Marriage, Incarceration, and Parenting: Intersections and Opportunities

The populations targeted by the Healthy Marriage Initiative and the SVORI and other reentry programs can overlap considerably. The majority of incarcerated individuals are parents, and of these, roughly a quarter are married and 46 percent were living with their children and presumably their child's mother at the time of their arrest.[1] Marital, cohabiting and parent-child relationships are at especially high risk of disruption when parents are involved in the criminal justice system. For those who want to continue their family relationships, there is currently little institutional support to assist the family.

In 2002, the Office of the Assistant Secretary for Planning and Evaluation (ASPE), in collaboration with SAMHSA and the National Institute for Child Health and Human Development, gathered stakeholders from the criminal justice and health and human services research and practice communities to discuss how children and families are affected by the incarceration of a parent. Research papers developed as a result of the *From Prison to Home: The Effects of Incarceration and Reentry on Children, Families, and Communities* conference highlighted in detail the challenges faced by the families of imprisoned individuals and the need for programs and policies focused on facilitating the incarceration and reentry process for couples, their children, and their communities.[2]

In FY 2006, ACF announced that it would spend an estimated $4 million of the Responsible Fatherhood funding authorized under the Deficit Reduction Act (DRA) for Responsible Fatherhood, Marriage, and Family Strengthening Grants for Incarcerated Fathers and their Partners (MFS). Eligible entities would implement programs that provide services to promote or sustain healthy marriage primarily to unmarried couples and married couples with children where one of the parents is incarcerated or has other substantial involvement with the criminal justice system, including recent release from prison, jail, probation, or parole. In addition to marriage strengthening activities, grantees also could work in other authorized activity areas that improve parenting and promote economic stability. Responsible Fatherhood MFS Grants are to be innovative, well- designed, and accessible to interested couples and must take into account the unique circumstance of incarcerated and formerly incarcerated fathers. These grants differ from other priority area grants in that they focus only on fathers who are currently or very recently under criminal justice supervision. Additionally, marriage activities are the primary focus of these grants, although parenting and/or employment services can also be provided in order to strengthen the viability of the family unit. These demonstration projects also are required to collaborate with domestic violence experts in the development of their programs.

MFS approaches must involve stakeholders from the criminal justice system, as well as include diverse community sectors (e.g., government, schools, faith-based communities, healthcare and businesses). Because the incidence of mental health and substance abuse problems is higher in this population than in the general population, applicants must be able to demonstrate how they will help clients connect to these service systems, even though payment for such services is beyond the scope of the resources available under this grant. Further, MFS approaches are to consider issues of couples separated by geography; the continuity of services between prison and the community; the integration of MFS services into existing reentry programs; linkages with other service approaches to families with an incarcerated parent (e.g., mentoring children of prisoners); and the risk factors that must be considered in program planning (e.g., domestic violence).

In October 2006, ACF announced the recipients of the MFS grants, as well as other awards included for funding outside this priority area. While not specifically focused on the incarcerated population, many of the 125 grantees for marriage strengthening and 100 grantees for responsible fatherhood awards will be undertaking initiatives that hold promise for application to this population.

Within the DHHS, ASPE, with funding from the ACF Office of Family Assistance, will administer an evaluation project to document program development and evaluate MFS grantee success, using experimental design methodologies when appropriate and feasible. In addition, as a part of this study, technical assistance will be provided to help grantees comply with the evaluation requirements.

Another ACF initiative that focuses on the intersection of incarceration and family support is the Mentoring Children of Prisoners (MCP) program. While not marriage- focused, the MCP grants do incorporate the broader family issues affecting incarcerated parents by supporting the creation and maintenance of one-on-one mentoring relationships between children of incarcerated parents and caring, supportive adult mentors. MCP is designed to be a community-based mentoring program in which children and youth, ages 4–18, are appropriately matched with an adult mentor, who has been screened and trained, for a one-on-one (one mentor and one youth), friendship- oriented mentoring relationship. Grants have been awarded to community and faith-based organizations to support the establishment and/or expansion of mentoring programs in communities with substantial numbers of children of incarcerated parents.

D. Research and Practice Symposium on Marriage and Incarceration

On April 20 and 21, 2006, ASPE convened a diverse group of experts with research and practice knowledge about incarceration and reentry, marriage strengthening, family processes, and domestic violence. The purpose of the *Research and Practice Symposium on Marriage and Incarceration* was to understand more fully the strategies for improving outcomes for couples who want to maintain healthy marriages during and after one of the partners is incarcerated. The symposium aimed to achieve the following:

- Increase understanding among the criminal justice and marriage education disciplines about how these issues are viewed on either side
- Identify practice needs and gaps in order to improve marriage outcomes for these couples
- Review research topics for improved understanding of the efficacy of various interventions for this population.

The focus of the 2-day discussion was on strength-based strategies to improve the marriages and family life of those incarcerated or returning from a period of incarceration. It was not intended to be a discussion of criminal justice reform. While criminal justice representatives were present at the symposium, along with members of the DOJ, academics, and health and human service providers, the DHHS was keen that marriage interventions be the primary focus of discussion; therefore, recommendations primarily centered on what additional research or components were needed to improve marriage education curricula and their delivery for this population.

ASPE asked several experts from across the disciplines of justice and incarceration, family and marriage, health, and social services to provide remarks about some of the key issues necessary to consider when examining or developing healthy marriage initiatives for this population group. These framing remarks were meant not to be all-encompassing but to help participants from across disciplines share their knowledge and to stimulate discussion of other issues critical to these programs. Summaries of these remarks are included as boxed text throughout this report to give context for the issues discussed.

The following chapters provide an overview of both the themes that emerged from the symposium and recommendations that can aid the direction of these types of programs and of future research. The next chapter highlights some of the contextual issues that must be taken into account in relation to working on marriage strengthening with this population. Chapter III looks at current practices that show promise for replication and further study and how these can be delivered in prisons and communities. Chapter IV discusses those gaps in knowledge that require further research and suggests possible strategies. The report concludes by discussing ways to move forward on research and practice that can support marriage and family relationships for currently and formerly incarcerated individuals.

Finally, it should be noted that this report is a summary of a conversation that took place among invited experts who came from different disciplines and held many different perspectives. It represents neither an overview of research findings nor government policy. It offers the opinions of a diverse group of experts trying to build a foundation of understanding about a complex social situation: families where an individual is disconnected from his spouse or partner and children due to incarceration.

In: Marriage and Incarceration
Editors: Leana H. Venten

ISBN: 978-1-60692-938-4

Chapter 2

CONTEXTUALIZING THE ISSUES

Brandy Bauer, Jamie Hart, Anne Hopewell and Naomi Tein
U.S. Department of Health and Human Services
Office of the Assistant Secretary for Planning and Evaluation

Experts were invited to provide context on the current prison environment, marriage education, domestic violence, and other issues relevant to the symposium. The purpose of these framing remarks was to stimulate discussion; the participants were not asked to come to a consensus on the most appropriate way to handle these issues, rather the issues were put "on the table" to inform the discussion.

This section reflects the lively presentations and discussion of the issues undertaken by the participants. The symposium organizers structured the agenda (see Appendix A) to focus on research and programming aimed at incarcerated men. While they acknowledged the myriad issues that also relate to female and juvenile offenders, it was thought that due to time constraints and because proposed solutions might be population- specific, it would be more appropriate to target one subgroup rather than the incarcerated population as a whole. Thus, the issues covered below speak specifically to the context of prison interventions for men, the largest group within the offender population.

A. The Prison Population

In order to identify programs targeted toward incarcerated individuals, it is important to understand who this audience is and their circumstances. The population of prisoners in Federal, State, and local jail facilities is a diverse one. According to data from the Bureau of Justice Statistics for 2004 (the most recent year for which full data are available), there were 1.5 million inmates in prisons and jails across the United States, and 95 percent of these will be released at some point in time. Women represented only seven percent of the total inmate population, and were more likely to be serving for drug-related offenses. Sixty percent of all inmates were African-American or Hispanic.[3]

More than half of all prison and jail inmates self-reported having a mental disorder, and these individuals also reported high incidences of co- occurring substance abuse problems. In the year prior to incarceration, 74 percent of State prisoners and 76 percent of local jail inmates reported being dependent on or abusing drugs or alcohol.[4]

The Prison Population at a Glance

- 1.5 million inmates in prisons and jails
- 95% will be released at some point in time
- 60% of inmates are African-American or Hispanic
- More than half of all inmates have a self-reported mental disorder
- More than half of all inmates are parents to children under 18
- 44% of fathers in State prisons lived with their children prior to incarceration
- 36% of parents in Federal prison and 23% of parents in State prison are currently married
- 40% of State prisoners reported weekly contact with their children, but 57% reported never having a personal visit with their children since admission

Source: Bureau of Justice Statistics

A majority of State and Federal prisoners (55 and 63 percent respectively) also are parents to children under 18. In 1999,[5] roughly 2.1 percent of all minors in the United States had an incarcerated parent, and a majority of these parents, like the prison population in general, were violent offenders. Nearly half of all imprisoned parents were African-American. Parents in Federal prisons were slightly more likely to be married than those in State facilities (36 and 23 percent respectively).[6] Prior to admission, roughly 44 percent of fathers in State prisons lived with their children, presumably with their child's mother if they were unmarried.[7] Once incarcerated, however, the majority had no personal visits from their children, though approximately 40 percent claimed to have some contact, usually by telephone or mail.[8]

B. Circumstances of Incarceration and Release

The External Environment

Before discussing the current physical and psychological environment within prisons, presenters at the symposium were quick to point out that many offenders emerge from environments where their health and well-being are not functioning at an optimal level, and it is these same environments to which they will eventually return.

Mapping of neighborhoods with high rates of incarceration has shown that the majority of offenders come from a small set of inner city neighborhoods characterized by racial segregation, substandard housing, high unemployment and a high dependence on the use of federally funded assistance programs to meet basic subsistence needs.[9] As noted above, these circumstances contribute to many individuals having substance abuse and mental health disorders prior to incarceration. The prison environment therefore is not the sole cause of problems facing prisoners upon release but can exacerbate existing problems and make reintegration that much more difficult.

The Prison Environment

Prisoners are incarcerated for a reason: they have committed a crime that society has determined to necessitate a curtailment of individual freedom through removal from the community and family. By their very nature, prisons are coercive and interfere with the maintenance of familial and other social networks. Speakers at the symposium noted that this is not a criticism of the criminal justice system; rather, these characteristics are a facet of incarceration around which marriage education interventions need to work. Effective programming in prisons and jails needs to take into account the circumstances that lead to incarceration as well as the environment of incarceration and its effects on individuals and their families.

The last three decades have witnessed an unprecedented increase in the number of people incarcerated in this country. As prisons and jails have been forced to handle overcrowding, their methods of controlling the incarcerated population have shifted from rehabilitation to "crowd management" and using more punitive measures to deal with prisoner behavior. The term "prisonization" has been used to apply to the changes and adjustments that occur in people's personalities and habits when they have had to adapt to incarcerated life.

Framing the Issues: The Prison Environment
Craig Haney, University of California Santa Cruz

Dramatic increases have been seen in the rates of incarcerated individuals over the last 20–30 years, and the rapid increase in the prison population provides numerous challenges to the criminal justice system and impacts the lives of thousands of incarcerated individuals and, by extension, their families. Prisons are not "nice" places, nor are they supposed to be; however, the crowded conditions of many facilities coupled with a philosophical move away from a rehabilitative model of incarceration means that there is limited availability of services (such as drug treatment and anger management) that might address the very behaviors prisoners need to change in order to return successfully to the community and family upon release. The criminal justice system is also challenged by the needs of many mentally ill individuals whose needs for services are often not met in the prison environment.

The psychological effects of the prison environment that most directly impact interpersonal relationships such as marriage and family include: dependence on institutional structures and procedures that control every aspect of prisoners' lives; hypervigilance wrought by distrust of other prisoners and staff; emotional overcontrol and psychological distancing; social withdrawal and isolation, which diminish skills needed to navigate the complexity of the world after release; diminished self-worth and personal value; and symptoms of posttraumatic stress disorder in some individuals.

These conditions are not uniformly distributed across all prison populations; African-American and Hispanic/Latino populations are overrepresented in prisons today and frequently experience post-prison adjustment reactions. In turn, these adjustment reactions negatively impact African- American and Hispanic/Latino families and the communities in which they live.

These shifting management styles have in turn altered the psychological environment of prisons. Prisonization requires dependency on the institution to rule and regulate every aspect of prisoners' lives. In response, prisoners may either withdraw emotionally or become hypervigilant of their surroundings. Upon release, the effects of living in such surroundings may manifest themselves in a variety of ways. Ex-offenders can face a host of emotional difficulties in adapting to life outside the prison, including low self-esteem or depression, distrust, hypervigilance, and posttraumatic stress disorder.

The prison environment likewise impedes the cultivation of healthy relationships with partners and children. There is an inherent lack of intimacy and privacy in prison settings, with many offenders unable even to touch their family members upon meeting. Similarly, as more prisoners are incarcerated in facilities far from their homes, their ability to maintain close relationships with family and friends is lessened and negatively affects their ability to cope with their environment.

Health and Well-Being

Compounding these psychological issues are often health problems associated with, or exacerbated by, incarceration. Infectious diseases such as HIV, tuberculosis, and hepatitis C occur widely among the imprisoned population. [10] In addition to impacting physical health, these conditions also can impact families and communities negatively and disproportionately upon release. This may be especially true for communities where there is little access to health services because few people have private health insurance or where public health systems or private limited coverage are inadequate. In low-income communities, children are generally covered by publicly financed services, but most adults are reliant on public health clinics and emergency room care.

A disproportionate share of the prison population also has existing issues related to substance abuse and mental health. Dependence on crack cocaine, alcohol, crystal methamphetamine, and other substances may go untreated, although there are promising programs that could be integrated into other interventions. Often, prisoners are dually diagnosed with substance abuse and mental health issues, compounding their service needs. Moreover, incarcerated individuals with undiagnosed or untreated mental illnesses or substance abuse problems also may not be able to form strong bonds with families and others.

Economics

These psychological and health concerns pose significant hurdles for reuniting families, and an additional challenge is the financial burden of imprisonment. Loss of income and child support, payment of court and lawyer fees and maintaining costs of prison-related expenses (e.g., phone calls) can be financially devastating to families, especially when they are low-income. These costs do not immediately go away upon release.

Reluctance to hire ex-offenders means that they face a lack of employment opportunities as well as delays in obtaining the resources to support their families. Being able to provide for one's family is a critical aspect of being a successful partner in a marriage. Felons are ineligible for Pell Grants and public housing and are excluded from many professions that require State licenses.

Framing the Issues: The Burden of Incarceration and Reunification
Creasie Finney Hairston, University of Illinois–Chicago

Maintaining a relationship when one partner is incarcerated is expensive. Some of the financial burdens on couples include loss of income and/or financial support of children, costs for bail and lawyers that often require putting up homes for collateral, costs associated with visiting, exorbitant rates for collect calls from prison, and prisoner requests for money for items the prison may not be providing.

Moreover, imprisonment creates an abnormal environment for an adult relationship and the wives and partners of imprisoned men are in essence "doing time" themselves. Incarceration is a "long-distance" relationship in both geographic and emotional terms and women can only see their husbands/partners when the prison allows. Social distance and lack of companionship can fray any strong emotional bond and incarceration fosters a lack of privacy for an adult relationship, including sexual intimacy.

Reunified couples face a number of challenges in creating successful marriages. Upon release, partners may have unrealistic expectations surrounding reunification, since it has been the topic of conversation throughout the period of incarceration. Couples in fragile relationships, in particular, have an especially hard time immediately before a prisoner is released. In some relationships, the wife/partner makes the decision to "make a clean break" before her partner returns. Should the relationship remain intact, the couple may face severe economic pressures, and women typically expect their partners to make a contribution to the financial well-being of the family despite the challenges a felon faces in obtaining employment.

Given that economic problems are a frequent source of conflict for all couples (including those with an incarcerated family member) and often the focus of marital breakup, marriage strengthening programs for this population need to recognize the additional strains imposed by incarceration on these marriages and families, and prepare them for this at all stages.

C. Domestic Violence

The role that domestic violence plays in the lives of incarcerated men and their families was discussed throughout the 2-day symposium as a critical issue to consider when talking about marriage education and responsible fatherhood programming for this population.

Framing the Issues: Typologies of Domestic Violence
Amy Holtzworth-Munroe, Indiana University/Bloomington

Rates of domestic violence vary across the country and have an impact on family/couple interactions. Domestic violence involves a range of behaviors from pushing and shoving to murder and not all batterers can or should be reunited with their partners.

When addressing domestic violence, it is critical to look at three levels: sociocultural influences, the particular family/couple and their interactions, and the individual. What is known is that there are varying degrees of violence, and men differ in their patterns – some may confine violent behavior to the context of a single relationship, whereas others may exhibit violence in all of their daily interactions. Other factors known to influence male violent behavior include substance abuse (with significant correlates between amount consumed and levels of violence), attitudes toward women, past trauma, deficits in cognition around how to best address a negative situation. Thus, there are several typologies that can be applied to battering interventions: one focuses on the individual man and his violence across interactions, while another focuses on "intimate terrorism" and the interactions of both men and women within a couple.

Women and children in domestic violence situations often perceive economics as a barrier to leaving the marriage. The data indicate that two-thirds of battered women eventually leave their situation, though often after five or more attempts. It is well-known that the most dangerous time for a woman is when she leaves, as this is when she is most likely to be killed. Women need to develop the skills and support network that will enable them to leave successfully. Even when they understand the risks, many women are committed to their relationships and want to remain with their partners, if the relationship can become nonviolent. This situation provides an opportunity for intervention. Unfortunately, two meta-analyses of battering programs indicate that battering programs are no more effective than arrest at reducing rates of violence.

Persons incarcerated for violent crimes may already have a high potential for that violence carrying over into domestic relationships; harsh prison conditions can exacerbate this tendency toward violence. Many marriage education programs that are implemented outside of the prison setting screen for domestic violence beforehand and do not allow couples with these issues to participate in the program. However, such screening may not feasible when dealing with the incarcerated, and therefore marriage education programs conducted with this population need to directly include domestic violence protocols.[11]

Framing the Issues: The Domestic Violence Safe Return Initiative
Oliver Williams, University of Minnesota

Many women stay in abusive relationships because they "love the batterer, not the abuse" and believe that change is possible. Thus we need to think of better ways to facilitate that. The question is, how does one engage men in the process of change?

The Domestic Violence Safe Return Initiative (www.vera.org, search under "safe return"), funded by the Department of Justice, is a demonstration program that works with formerly incarcerated men to change their violent behaviors so they can return home. These men want to change, often so that they can be good fathers to their children. However, the goal should not be marriage and fatherhood at all costs but that transformation is indeed possible for some. The testimonials of former batterers and the research being done on this program may lead to further insights on how best to treat these men and reunite them with their families.

Service providers and case managers must support the idea that relationship classes, such as marriage education, early intervention, training, and support that lessen the economic barriers can be productive interventions. This initiative strives to "birth the truth" about being a responsible man, husband, and father and emphasizes the need not to pass the violence on to children but to create peace in families. Practitioners working with these men must understand the real issues of racism and stigma that they face on a daily basis. The Safe Return Initiative also works to find spiritual rather than religious ways to reach these men and transform their lives.

In order for violent men to address their behaviors successfully, a number of pieces must be in place, namely a decision to be "sober from violence", a seamless system of intervention, good probation and parole staff, skill building and transition classes in prisons, links to the community upon release, and church-based support. These elements, coupled with compassionate mentors who have lived the experience and can testify to their changed lives, are pieces that are necessary for change to occur. Such change is difficult to achieve but not impossible, and breaking the chain of violence can have long-term positive effects on families and communities.

Some participants at the symposium felt strongly that, for batterers and their partners, marriage education programs should focus less on the promotion of marriage than on building healthy relationships and giving these couples the tools that will ensure that violence has no place in their relationships, whether they have long-term commitment or not.

Most studies indicate that two- thirds of women eventually will leave a seriously violent relationship, though it may take several incidences of leaving and returning before a final break is made. Yet women are most vulnerable to severe battering and death during the time in which they attempt to leave. There are those women, however, who would prefer to remain in their relationship if it can become a nonviolent one, and programming should address their needs as well. Studies have demonstrated that women are more likely to stay when a batterer is in counseling, so for the incarcerated, this needs to happen prior to release.

Thus one of the major concerns for marriage education initiatives aimed at the incarcerated should be how to integrate a "do no harm" approach. Key to this is an emphasis on the safety of women and helping them to realize that sometimes, even if men change, the relationship cannot be salvaged and that women cannot assume responsibility for the success or failure of an intervention.

Other considerations regarding integrating domestic violence into marriage strengthening programs include:

- How to integrate comprehensive services to address other underlying problems (e.g., substance abuse, mental health services)
- How to ensure that men break the cycle of emotional and psychological control in addition to physical abuse
- How to integrate children into programming to mitigate the negative effects of violence on their lives.

Involving domestic violence experts in the early stages of developing and implementing marriage education curricula is seen as a positive first step to addressing these concurrent issues.

D. Racism and Cultural Competency

A disproportionate share of individuals currently incarcerated are people of color. Minority communities encounter a number of societal difficulties, including high rates of poverty, more children growing up in single-parent families, and, among African- Americans, lower rates of marriage overall. Yet minority populations have largely been left out of large scale research projects examining the factors that contribute to recidivism and transformation, and many interventions lack the cultural competency needed to address these circumstances.

Participants noted that racism exacerbates the issues around incarceration and reentry for people of color. Incarceration disproportionately affects people and communities of color since racial minorities are more likely to be imprisoned. For example, mandatory sentencing, especially for crack cocaine, negatively impacts many African-American families and communities. Additionally, participants noted that racism makes reentry into the community and the workforce more challenging. It is difficult for all ex-offenders to reestablish paid employment and support their families, but participants pointed out that because of racism, particularly in the hiring process, this can be even more difficult for men of color. Thus, incarceration can limit life opportunities severely for some men and can challenge ideas of manhood, especially the conceptualization of men as family providers and protectors, participants observed. Racism also can set up expectations of failure for ex-offenders that make recidivism an even greater likelihood.

Participants expressed concern that we do not know how this issue of disproportional rates of incarceration and other criminal justice involvement interacts with marriage. Marriage has been decreasing in many communities at the same time that rates of incarceration have been increasing. Do incarceration and criminal records make it less likely that an individual marries? It may also be that not marrying increases the likelihood that an individual may be more likely to engage in activities that lead to incarceration. Whatever the directions of causality, incarceration and other types of criminal justice involvement may add to the difficulties people of color experience in fulfilling the responsibilities associated with marriage, especially financial support, and thus may make it less likely for these individuals to marry or to stay married.

The need for cultural competency among all those delivering interventions was stressed by symposium participants. Prisoners are more apt to respond to someone who can understand "where they're coming from" and the value of peer counseling, sincerity, and cultural competency were noted as the skills needed to transcend issues of race and gender when delivering services.

In: Marriage and Incarceration
Editors: Leana H. Venten
ISBN: 978-1-60692-938-4

Chapter 3

THE CURRENT STATE OF PRACTICE

Brandy Bauer, Jamie Hart, Anne Hopewell and Naomi Tein
U.S. Department of Health and Human Services
Office of the Assistant Secretary for Planning and Evaluation

A. EMERGING PRACTICES IN MARRIAGE EDUCATION

The relative newness of programs aimed at strengthening marriages and families affected by incarceration means that, to date, there has been little comprehensive evaluation of these programs and their long-term effects on reducing recidivism. Nevertheless, the participants at the symposium shared preliminary evidence from the field that does point to early successes in certain areas that may be worthy of replication and further study across different populations and environments. Marriage education for this population can be informed by other marriage education efforts directed at low-income and minority populations, as well as by other family strengthening programs targeted at populations under criminal justice supervision or at risk of incarceration. It should be noted that there was no consensus among the participants on which practices were most effective, and many of these examples were countered with the caveat that all need to be studied in greater depth.

Framing the Issues: Adapting a Marriage – Strengthening Curriculum for the Incarcerated

Howard Markman, Center for Marital and Family Studies, University of Denver

The Prevention and Relationship Enhancement Program (PREP) marriage-strengthening curriculum is being used by the Oklahoma Department of Human Services' Oklahoma Marriage Initiative. While the original PREP curriculum was not designed for use with prison populations, the program was redesigned to include additional and different materials for the prison context. In Oklahoma, PREP Inside and Out focuses on communication skills, commitment, negative effect management, respect, mate selection, aggression, positive connections, and commitment, with emphasis on the unique issues faced by prisoners and their partners.

PREP Inside and Out is not a reentry program; rather, it is a faith-based program whereby individuals who may soon be released or not are given an opportunity to transform their core belief systems. In the Oklahoma program, trained chaplains meet with a voluntary group of couples during the time when one partner is incarcerated. This version of the course is delivered though a 12-hour program over 6 weeks with 2 hours per session (although the PREP course can range up to a 30-hour intervention). During this time, couples learn to talk without fighting, listen actively, manage finances, and raise children.

Pre- and postevaluations of the program indicate that of 177 male prisoners in the Inside and Out program in a medium-security Oklahoma prison, 162 were in relationships. Of these, 40 percent were married. The self- report measures after participation in the program noted that negative interaction decreased, communication skills increased, relationship satisfaction for both partners improved, and loneliness decreased overall. A 30-day followup study indicated that the benefits were maintained is lasting.

While there is still little marriage education aimed specifically at the incarcerated population, there are preliminary lessons to be learned from the first attempts at such programs (such as the adaptation of the Prevention and Relationship Enhancement Program to prison settings, highlighted in the box), as well as marriage education within broader society.

Marriage education can be implemented with individuals as well as with couples in a variety of settings, and it works best when rooted in the research about what makes a marriage healthy. The Building Strong Families project[12] notes that there is a wide variety of existing marriage education curricula focused around the following content areas: developing empathy, communication, and conflict management skills; building fondness, affection, and emotional intimacy; identifying signs of relationship or marital meltdown; managing parenthood; and enhancing parent-infant relationships (especially fatherhood). These topics are of relevance to all couples, including incarcerated families, and many couples – both inside and outside of prison settings – have noted anecdotally improvements in these areas and more satisfaction with their marriage after participation.

Framing the Issues: Marriage Education and the African- American Community

Lorraine Blackman, Indiana University School of Social Work

A number of societal challenges have worked against the strengthening of African-American families over the past several decades. At the end of the Vietnam War, many fathers returned traumatized by war, suffering from posttraumatic stress disorder, which often co-occurred with substance use issues. This coincided with a reduction of available jobs for men with low education levels, meaning former soldiers often had difficulty sustaining a family financially. In the 1980s, the advent of crack cocaine further contributed to the breakdown of stability in African- American families.

Decades later, because of these societal shifts intervention is needed in many of these communities, and marriage education is an important component of transforming communities. However, key to the success of healthy marriage programming is working with healthy functioning people, but rarely are those entering and exiting prison without other significant problems. Thus, marriage education is not a substitute for addressing issues of substance abuse, domestic violence, or mental illness, and marriage education should be one of a range of programs offered to incarcerated individuals and families.

Anyone working within African-American communities must also take into consideration the following:

- Influence of gang culture
- Lack of employed role models
- Children often with different partners (multiple partner fertility)
- Cultural de-emphasis on marriage
- Concerns about fidelity and HIV status.

Many African-American women would like to marry but have no partners available, in part because of the high rates of incarceration. Therefore, marriage education curricula may need to be modified to meet the unique needs of African-American and other minority families and communities.

Table 1. Marriage Education Content Areas and Relevance for Incarcerated Individuals and Their Families.

Content Area	Goals	Relevance to Incarcerated Couples
Developing empathy, communication and conflict management	Effective communication and empathy are crucial to healthy interpersonal relationships	Applicable to all couples, regardless of situation
Building fondness, affection and emotional intimacy	Affection and intimacy build relationships beyond merely communicating well	Applicable to all couples, regardless of situation
Identifying signs of relationship and marital meltdown	Helping couples see how criticism and defensive behaviors contribute to erosion of relationships	Applicable to all couples, regardless of situation
Managing parenthood and enhancing parent-infant relations	Helping couples recognize the changes that parenthood bring to relationships and to assume equal partner-ship in child rearing	Applicable to all couples, regardless of situation
Considering marriage	Education on benefits of marriage and how to put relationships first	Research indicates that many couples – including one with an incarcerated partner – do want to get married
Managing complex family relationships	Addressing multi-parent fertility and extended families and how they impact on relationships	BJS statistics indicate that many incarcerated parents have complex family relationships, often with children by several different partners
Building mutual trust and commitment	Engaging couples in discussions where they set criteria for committed relationships	Trust may be eroded after exposure to prison environment and long separation from partner

Content Area	Goals	Relevance to Incarcerated Couples
Managing stress and emotions	Teaching couples to avoid situations that can lead to violence against their partners or children	Violence permeates many communities that have disproportionate numbers of offenders
Managing and communicating about family finances	Providing training in financial management	Applicable to all couples, regardless of situation, though ex-offenders may face increased difficulties with obtaining employment and accessing financial services upon release
Enhancing marriage-ability through family support services	Offering education, training, job assistance, child care, domestic violence treatment and substance abuse treatment to address those challenges which impede formation of healthy marriages and families	Offenders and their families are of increased likelihood to come from low-income, lower-education backgrounds and have problems with substance abuse and mental health

Table 1 illustrates those content areas that projects such as Building Strong Families and Supporting Healthy Marriage[13] acknowledge should be included in marriage education but should remain somewhat limited in the curricula at this time.[14] These include managing complex family relationships, stress, trust, and communication around finances, as well as connecting to other services. Several participants at the symposium noted that the most promising aspect of marriage education is that it "can open the door to seeking services in other domains." By exposing people to messages about healthy behaviors in marriage, marriage education also can reiterate messages aimed at transforming other aspects of life, prompting participants to seek, for example, substance abuse treatment and other interventions they might require.

As a part of its Healthy Marriage Initiative, ACF has developed three population-specific initiatives focused on marriage education and promotion among minorities. These initiatives are the African-American Healthy Marriage Initiative, the Hispanic Healthy Marriage Initiative and the Native American Health Marriage Initiative. These initiatives were developed in recognition of the concern that marriage education, like other programs and service delivery mechanisms, may be more effective if presented in ways that reflect the culture of the target communities. Each of the three initiatives promotes culturally competent strategies to address healthy marriage formation and responsible fatherhood amid the unique cultural, demographic, and socioeconomic factors affecting these communities. Because rates of incarceration are very high in some minority communities, these population specific components of the Healthy Marriage Initiative will have specific relevance to marriage education activities focused on incarcerated individuals and their families.

B. Other Strategies That Support Family Strengthening

In addition to marriage education programs specifically, other strategies were cited by symposium participants as having application to interventions aimed at strengthening families and marriages (Table 2). Like marriage education, these interventions focus on assisting people with the building the foundation of healthy relationships: they support personal growth (such as addressing underlying illnesses and addictions) and responsibility, provide opportunities to strengthen the parent-child bond, and support offenders with seeking out services such as employment that can help offer stability to their partners and families.

- ***Early intervention.*** Some participants at the symposium cited the need for more replication of preprison activities that aim to influence vulnerable populations away from criminal behavior. Early intervention strategies, particularly targeting youth, that have shown some initial positive outcomes include bringing ex- convicts into schools and community centers for dialogue, as well as using other media to illustrate the negative aspects of imprisonment. These interventions can, in addition to steering youth away from criminality, reinforce messages about maintaining positive relationships and the importance of fathers playing an active role in child rearing.

- ***Practices within the prison setting.*** A number of practices occurring within the prison setting also were raised as promising strategies. Several States are using level-of-service inventories (LSI) upon intake to assess how prisoners fit along a continuum of factors – from substance abuse and mental health issues to family relationships – and to determine their risks for re-offending after release. The LSI works only when there are services in place to address problems identified during the intake process, and resources to assist prisoners with overcoming challenges throughout their imprisonment.

The establishment of prison facilities that resemble halfway houses and give offenders the opportunity to move away from prisonization was also identified as a practice that can ease the transition from prison to community. However, several criminal justice experts noted that a problem with the current justice system is not knowing approximate release dates of prisoners and having adequate time to transition them to such facilities before they go home.

- ***Family interventions.*** Numerous family interventions also provide examples of how services can work with more than the incarcerated individual to ease the transition of release. Some of these try to involve the entire family in a spectrum of services for the offender (e.g., substance abuse treatment), to encourage healing and recovery for all members. Others assign case managers or mentors to work with families on the transition process.

- ***Work with children.*** Some programs focus solely on children with incarcerated parents. These include programs that facilitate prison visits to strengthen the parent-child bond or provide mentoring to decrease risky behavior by providing positive attention and role models. The DHHS discretionary grant program, Mentoring Children of Prisoners, is an example of a large scale effort to identify and provide mentors for children with incarcerated parents. Likewise, child support diversion programs help to encourage incarcerated and released fathers to do right by supporting their children without threatening them with further jail time for inability to meet fully their financial obligations.

- ***Reintegration activities.*** The need to continue serving prisoners after release was highlighted a number of times, and there are a few existing interventions that have shown some success at getting ex-offenders reintegrated into their communities. Chief among these is connecting people to jobs. Because obtaining employment is such a challenge for ex-offenders, employment and mentoring programs can provide a valuable support to link these individuals with employers willing to hire them and provide emotional support as they work to provide for themselves and their families. Faith-based programs that work within and outside the prison setting also can offer a valuable support to offenders and assist them with accessing services upon release.

Table 2. Other Strategies with Application to Marriage Strengthening Initiatives.

Strategy	Target Population	Goals	Examples *
LSI	Offenders just entering prison	Assessing static factors (e.g., health, family status, substance use) to predict risk and likelihood of recidivism; enables social workers and coordinators to prepare inmates for release through targeted interventions	Used by a number of State correctional facilities (e.g., Iowa, Oklahoma)
Early intervention	Vulnerable youth and communities	Targeting people preprison to impress upon them the severity of prison and that incarceration is not a "rite of passage"	Videos like Doing Time; ex-convicts who can do presentations in communities
Faith-based approaches	Incarcerated individuals	Recognizing that many prisoners trust prison chaplains and faith leaders, these approaches collaborate with existing faith programs within prisons to deliver messages and services	Prison Fellowship Ministry; programs that include mentoring such as the DOL-funded PRI grants
Strategy	Target Population	Goals	Examples *
Family interventions	Families of incarcerated persons	Identifying family needs and targeting services to ease	Programs working with specific communities (e.g.,

		transition; integrating wide range of resources	La Bodega de la Familia, CURE)
Mentoring children	Children of incarcerated parents	Encouraging positive behavior among at-risk youth; streng-thening the parent-child bond with parent in prison	DHHS-funded Mentoring Children of Prisoners Program (MCP); Girl Scouts Behind Bars
Employment mentoring	Newly released ex-offenders	Linking offenders with willing business owners who provide jobs and support during transition	Safer Foundation, Chicago; and the Center for Employ-ment Opportu-nities (CEO), New York City
Child support and paternity establishment	Incarcerated individuals with children	Aiming to get prisoners to acknowledge their role as parents and provide emotional and (where possible) financial support to them	Diversion programs (e.g., Alexandria, VA) that assist incar-cerated and newly released offenders with supporting children and not going into arrears for failure to pay child support
Halfway-house facilities	Prisoners to be released in near future	Giving prisoners an opportunity to adapt to more freedoms and begin make decisions in less restrictive environment	Some examples within State correctional facilities (e.g., New Jersey, Pennsylvania)

Participants at the symposium noted that the "success" of many of these practices deemed to be promising is based on either self-report or short-term followup. For those interventions that are individual focused, the self-report may be an accurate reflection of perceived benefits, but it is not able to assess whether the intervention benefited the family beyond the individual. To accurately gauge the success of an intervention aimed at reducing recidivism and keeping healthy marriages intact, long-term followup of families is needed. Proposed studies, as well as other research needs related to these practices, are covered in the next chapter of this report.

C. Delivery Options

Chief suggestions regarding delivery options for marriage education involved reliance on faith-based groups and spiritual personnel (chaplains) working inside the prison setting. Prison chaplains are an integral part of the prison environment, and an often trusted source of guidance for prisoners. Working collaboratively with chaplains can reach those individuals wanting to make positive transformations in their lives, especially because they can continue to do followup on site.

Beyond prison chaplaincies, however, it was noted that external faith-based groups often have a prison outreach program and are keen to work with this population. Some of these groups already train people to go into prisons and work with prisoners, but faith-based groups might also be a key resource for assisting with postrelease programming, such as providing support for employment and finding housing.

Other comments about service delivery reflected the idea that the prison environment is also important to consider. Since both positive and negative reinforcement can come through the peer culture, it is crucial to look at who is selected to participate in programs, and the prison "community" they live in. Suggestions to target programming to an entire ward or cellmates were raised, with the point that men who are undergoing similar transformations can provide support for one another.

As noted in Chapter 2, cultural competency is key to service delivery of marriage education. Any intervention must draw upon the recognition that minority families face additional difficulties to building healthy relationships that have resulted from decades of racism, and must be sensitive to cultural mores. Conducting needs assessments, getting community feedback, and involving individuals and families in the design of interventions were all cited as culturally competent strategies that could be used in marriage education interventions.

Finally, the practitioners at the symposium noted that the mode of delivery is as important as the message for marriage education and other prison interventions. An emphasis on humor and "edutainment" was mentioned, as well as the need for learning to be kinesthetic and interactive, with appropriate follow-through and followup. Peer-to-peer delivery tends to work best, and cultural competency must underlie all interventions.

D. Community Support Mechanisms

Participants agreed that communities can provide social and economic support critical to the success of this population. They then highlighted various community mechanisms and resources integral to supporting a healthy marriage in which one individual is or has been incarcerated (Figure 1).

While many of these resources draw upon traditional private community groups (such as nonprofits and other organizations), the concept of "community mechanisms" used by the symposium participants was considered broadly to also include public services such as probation and social welfare programs.

- Probation
- Parole (e.g., training parole officers as TANF workers to address multiple issues within the target population)
- Churches (during and after incarceration)
- Employment organizations
- Public services – TANF, SSI
- Coalitions – broad support
- Drug-free reentry coalitions
- Foster care/adoption
- Diversion/youth services
- Child support services

Figure 1. Public and Private Community Support Mechanisms

On the preprison side, probation was seen as a potential way in which programs could be introduced to vulnerable populations in order to reduce the likelihood that they will commit crimes that lead to prison. Probation is also a way to keep families intact (thereby reducing the stress of separation caused by incarceration). Notably, however, these programs need to be voluntary to probationers and they must not feel coerced into participation.

The issue of child support also was observed to be an area where more community support is needed. More work needs to be done to support men in providing for their children, and not running away from fatherhood responsibilities, regardless of whether they are in long-term relationships with the children's mother. Some States look upon incarceration as "voluntary unemployment" and child support bills add up; later on, being in arrears can be a felony offense itself. Alternate ways to design child support programs should be considered for the prison parent population that encourages them to do their familial duty but doesn't unjustly penalize them further for being incarcerated.

Diversion programs for child support were cited as one mechanism that could be used for prisoners after release that would encourage them to support their children without facing jail time for back payment. Participants also mentioned diversion programs for individuals with histories of domestic violence and substance abuse, though noting that these haven't proven successful yet for this population.

Places of worship (e.g., churches, mosques and synagogues) can be another form of support both to incarcerated men and their families by connecting them to services upon their release. Because faith-based organizations also can be used to deliver marriage education programs, they can offer a full spectrum of support for families making the transition from prison to home.

Another support for children of the incarcerated is community organizations such as Big Brothers/Big Sisters, Girl and Boy Scouts and Girls and Boys Clubs. These can reach out to children affected by incarceration and provide mentoring and modeling of appropriate behavior.

Recognizing the strain that can occur within families and relationships when basic subsistence needs go unmet, participants also listed a range of community services that can help released offenders meet basic needs of housing, food and employment. These include: TANF (food stamps), SSI, vocational rehabilitation organizations, State and county collaborations around reentry and work release, and institutions that can assist with licensing and employment.

It was thought that these community mechanisms work best when organizations can do "double duty" – i.e., address multiple issues affecting the individual. For example, employment programs can talk about parenting issues, TANF workers can assist with connecting to marital relationship services, etc. This approach, as well as coalitions of organizations working together for this population, can reinforce messages about strengthening marriage and families, but they work best when there is mapping of needs and resources within communities.

Some of the challenges facing these community support mechanisms is the need to train or cross-train professionals in meeting the myriad needs of ex-offenders, and helping them to handle large caseloads. Another problem is fighting resistance in communities to serving offenders, who can be perceived as dangerous. One proposed solution to this problem was better public education – creating public service announcements, for instance, that educate people about the prison environment and understand how to help people transition back into society.

In: Marriage and Incarceration
Editors: Leana H. Venten
ISBN: 978-1-60692-938-4

Chapter 4

What We Still Need to Know

Brandy Bauer, Jamie Hart, Anne Hopewell and Naomi Tein
U.S. Department of Health and Human Services
Office of the Assistant Secretary for Planning and Evaluation

While there are huge gaps in knowledge related to prisoners, their relationships, and factors contributing to the successful reintegration into communities, the symposium participants did acknowledge that there are some key findings we do know from the research. Longitudinal studies of ex-reform school offenders conducted by Dr. John Laub of the University of Maryland-College Park, for example, have shown that the best predictors of not recidivating were strong ties to a spouse and work. Likewise, other research highlighted at the meeting around personal transformation and motivation can provide insight into how offenders can mend relationships and not reoffend. Nevertheless, how these factors apply to marriage education within the prison setting is still largely unknown.

A. Research Needs for Marriage Education

One major concern among the symposium participants was that those practices that seem to suggest promising results for strengthening marriages for this population have not been evaluated yet. The participants strongly emphasized the need to know more about practices and what really works longterm. Another concern was that while there is research on marriage and research on incarceration, there is little targeted research looking at the intersection of these. Other data necessary to move forward include more on demographics of prisoners' families, family variables, the delivery of interventions, identity development, and the cost-benefits of such programming. These discussions are described below and presented in summary form in Table 3.

More Data on Prisoners and the Prison Environment

While there are many datasets breaking down the prison population by age, race, and type of crime, more demographic data are needed related to prisoners' backgrounds and family lives. Specifically:

- What percentage of marriages break up when one partner is incarcerated?
- What percentage of relationships are formed in prisons?
- What are the differences by gender for these statistics?
- What is the breakdown of prisoners who are parents or married by type of crime committed (violent vs. drug or other offense)?
- Of those fathers who are no longer involved with their children's mother, how many maintain relationships with their children?
- What about multiparent fertility – how many fathers who have children by different mothers have relationships with all of their children (or some, and which children)?

More information is sought regarding the different types of prisons or programs that prisoners come out of, and how these affect outcomes. Are the successes noted among those participating in healthy marriage/relationship and other programs being released after a long or short period in prison, and from what types of facilities are they emerging? How can the period from intake to release be used to influence attitudes and behaviors? Increasingly, prisons may "specialize" in an area, such as substance abuse treatment, or may be a faith-based prison; what research exists regarding these facilities and the success rates for those coming out of them?

In what ways do prisoners themselves understand how incarceration may have impacted their social, psychological, and emotional well-being and what can they do to mitigate these effects?

Framing the Issues: Research and Practice Knowledge Needs: Suggestions from the Field
Randy Day, Brigham Young University

Current research has not focused on African-Americans, and perhaps policies and programming would be different if the prison population was not disproportionately African-American. The implications of this lack of specificity on issues such as race are not known and solid programming should be based on research as opposed to preexisting curricula and policy.

There is strong research evidence that men do better when there is a connection to family. However, not much is known about the preexisting conditions of the family profiles of the men studied (strength, commitment, trust, prior family orientation before the individual entered prison), which challenges researchers to conduct more careful exploration in advance and look at what kind of constructs are being considered. Studies conducted during incarceration are easier to implement, since cases are easy to track and qualitative information is easy to obtain, as opposed to the challenge of tracking people after they are released from prison. However, some research study designs within prisons are limited by the Institutional Review Board process, which aims to protect prisoners who participate in research and may find the incentive of paying for prisoners' participation coercive or unfair in accordance with prison rules.

A greater investment in youth services and consideration of family-level variables are also needed. People who have gone to prison are showing up in some of the large datasets, such as the National Longitudinal Study of Youth 1979, which now has 20 years of data from 10,000 families across the United States. Using a family services supplement model, families that get into trouble can be predicted and the prison experience can be tracked.

Family Variables

Several participants noted that in prison programming, much work has been done at the individual level to address personal issues (e.g., substance abuse, depression), but little is being done on a family level. Are there family-level measurements that can be applied when looking at these programs?

One of the major problems in measuring families' variables is the complicated nature of many family relationships. Many incarcerated men who are fathers may have multiple children with different women, and varying relationships with them, or may view cohabitation as the equivalent of marriage. How can these relationships be strengthened when they are not clearly defined? What additional insight is needed to intervene in cultures or communities where the meaning of "relationship" or "marriage" does not reflect that of the dominant society? Moreover, do the complex relationships found in families with children from different fathers residing in the same household impact family income and social outcomes for the children of incarcerated fathers?

Framing the Issues: Research and Practice Knowledge Needs: Suggestions from the Field
Robert Lerman, Urban Institute

Economic measures and cost-benefit analysis should be used to determine what interventions were most effective. With regard to marriage education, the potential impacts could be measured on how much is saved/earned/accumulated by couples staying married for 5 years or how stable marriages impact children. If we change one couple, what is that worth in terms of increased earning potential, reduced recidivism, improved earning potential, and enhanced life satisfaction? The benefits of marriage education can be very substantial, especially if positive results can be replicated. Research on whether an intervention is generalizable and how to determine the costs and benefits are worth testing.

Since culture looks for short-term solutions, developing research guidelines, conducting prospective cost-benefit analysis, and investigating the implications for replication are problematic. As researchers and practitioners, can there be a common agreement on terms and outcomes? Marriage education starts with recognizing the realities of the lives of these couples while maintaining modest expectations for positive results. The cost savings of reaching even a few couples and their children are significant.

By capitalizing on the opportunities presented by individuals who are willing to be transformed, incremental change toward a common vision is possible. Society should begin to think strategically about prevention. Reducing prisonization is making a positive difference – and as partners, we should take the steps needed to bring about change for incarcerated men, their wives, and their families.

Little too is understood about parental relationships. For those fathers who want to be involved in their children's lives, what are the criteria that affect how they prioritize those relationships? Moreover, how do incarcerated men parent their children? More needs to be understood about the types of men and crimes they commit (violent or nonviolent) as it pertains to parenting. Do nonparenting programs (e.g., domestic violence, marriage education) have any effect on parenting, to make it more supportive, more responsive? Do prison visitation experiences and/or video conferences between fathers and their children serve to strengthen families and improve outcomes for at-risk children, especially vulnerable adolescents? How best can the intergenerational nature of crime be broken?

Research into the incidence of domestic violence among the incarcerated was also raised as a need. Are there correlates between types of crimes arrested for and the propensity for violence in the home? What are the rates of violence against partners versus violence against children or all members of the family? Does reducing crime in the first place in turn reduce domestic violence?

Program Design and Delivery

Prisoners who participate in marriage strengthening or parenting programs while incarcerated don't do so in a vacuum – their past and current living environments continue to influence their behavior even as they receive messages and positive reinforcement from these programs. One question of concern is how to "nest" these programs within prison communities. If the prison environment does not support the behavior changes indicated by such programs, how can they be implemented to better ensure success? Are there ways of conducting interventions (e.g., cell mates participating together in programs, targeting programs to residents in certain dormitories) that mitigate the prison environment negating the successes of those interventions? What opportunities exist prior to the prison setting – within juvenile justice, jail sentences, probation, and parole – to intervene earlier in the lives of individuals and families at risk?

Participants noted that the current study of the SVORI programs doesn't look at family transition. Are there other models (e.g., from the military) that can be studied for possible application to the incarcerated population? With those family-oriented programs that are offered in prisons, in what ways do they help reduce infractions by prisoners within that setting and recidivism when they get out? Likewise, what other tools exist that can be used within the prison setting to assist families with the transition process?

Another key area to examine related to delivering interventions is how to get messengers to work collaboratively with prison staff to get messages reinforced. Are there particular avenues, such as using prison chaplain services that are more effective than others?

Identity Theories and Resilience

One of the major set of questions raised at the symposium was around the mindset of offenders – from their choices that led to incarceration to their efforts to reform and keep from reoffending. Many participants felt that social scientists need to understand what risks contribute to criminality and incarceration in the first place. Specifically, how are incarcerated men different from other men and what selective influences affected their choices and therefore might impact their ability to respond to programming upon release?

Research on stages of change in other populations (e.g., people quitting smoking, losing weight, overcoming substance abuse) describes how people move from the stage of pre-contemplation – i.e., knowing you have got a problem but not wanting to change – to contemplation of change. This is the critical juncture when people get to the action phase; at the action phase, the type of intervention is not nearly as important as getting people to do something and learn from it. Then the person evolves into the more difficult maintenance phase.

Self-selection is critical to success, as it indicates readiness to change. Yet currently, there is very little research that even looks at the notion of identity theory, especially related to transformation, among this population. Likewise, while the research on recidivism is sparse, there is even less understanding of desistance and those men who have managed not to reenter the criminal justice system. Questions to be explored in this area include the following:

- What are the existing attitudes held by imprisoned men regarding their relationships, fatherhood, and their perceived life after prison?
- How does the experience of incarceration affect identity development?
- What characteristics are present in those men who do manage to transform their lives?
- What external influences have the most positive effects on those men who did successfully transition out of prison and back into their communities? Can these be integrated into prison programs?

Cost-Benefit Analyses and Other Outcomes

In addition to the data needs outlined above, participants also discussed cost-benefit analyses as a way to demonstrate the possible success of prison interventions. Prospective cost-benefit analyses are often done in the environmental arena, and can be adapted to the social sciences. For example, in the marriage education area, the unit costs of a program are relatively clear, and there is some literature on what potential impacts might be. The issue then is to assign value to these impacts. So, for example, one impact might be to sustain a marriage for more than 5 years and then to assess the impact of that on recidivism, on hours worked and wage rates, and stimulation of more labor market activity. There is other available research on how marriage affects children. When these impacts are given value, then researchers can assess the benefits of a couple not splitting up and perhaps the man returning to a somewhat constructive life, etc., and thereby can assign value to the programming that helped contribute to these outcomes. Such analyses can look at which interventions are most effective and make a case for continued funding of these.

Evaluation of Interventions

As mentioned in the previous chapter of this report, there is little comprehensive assessment of current programs and no long-term research on their efficacy. Participants at the symposium were emphatic that further evaluation of a range of programs – from screening tools, to marriage education and domestic violence interventions – be assessed in depth and that evaluation be included in program design. Questions to consider include:

Table 3. Summary of Potential Research Questions.

Understanding Prisoners and the Prison Environment
• What percentage of marriages break up in prison? (For men versus women?) • What percentages of relationships are formed in prisons? • What factors contribute to the ability of some prisoners to remain in relationships while incarcerated? • How many men maintain relationships with their children when they are no longer involved with the child's mother? When they have children by multiple partners? • How can the period from intake to release be used to influence attitudes and behaviors? • Are there differences in the impact of medium or maximum security prisons on inmates and their families? For example, does time served in minimum-security prisons and jails result in different outcomes? • In what ways do effective programs increase the understanding of prisoners on how incarceration may have impacted their social, psychological, and emotional well-being and how that relates to their interpersonal relationships?

Table 3. (Continued)

Family Variables
• How can we strengthen relationships that aren't clearly defined? What additional insight is needed to intervene in cultures or communities where the meaning of "relationship" or "marriage" does not reflect that of the dominant society? • How do incarcerated men parent their children? Does the nature of the crime committed reflect in any way on the nature of the parent-child relationship and how parenting is viewed? • Do prison visitation experiences and/or video conferences between fathers and their children serve to strengthen families and improve outcomes for at-risk children, especially vulnerable adolescents? How best can the intergenerational nature of crime be broken? • Do the complex relationships found in fragile and blended families with children from different fathers residing in the same household impact family income and social outcomes for the children of incarcerated fathers? • If there is a linkage between the absence of fathers and the likelihood of incarceration, what can be done to strengthen the relationship between sons and their incarcerated fathers? • Does the existence of prison industry enhancement increase self-esteem due to the payment of child support and increase consequently the likelihood of family unification or reunification?
Family Variables
• Can insights gained from domestic violence research be extrapolated to indicate which interventions best could minimize conflict for the relationships and families in which a partner experienced incarceration?
Program Design and Delivery
• Are voluntary programs or services (without the incentive of early release or other enticements) more effective than mandated ones for individuals who are incarcerated? • How much does the prison environment thwart the effectiveness of programming, and are there ways of conducting interventions that mitigate the prison environment negating their successes? • What other transitional programs, such as services currently available to military families facing the return of soldiers, could be effective and transferable to this population? • Family programs currently operating in the prisons should be studied to measure whether they decrease infractions of the participating prisoners. Do these programs reduce recidivism? What interventions best can maintain vibrant family relationships? How can family ties be strengthened during incarceration? • Do any tools exist that can help triage families and refer them to appropriate

services? Is the LSI the most effective tool? What can be done at intake to enable coordinators to prepare inmates, families, and communities for both the period of incarceration and the release?

- What opportunities exist within juvenile justice, jail sentences, probation, and parole to intervene earlier in the lives of individuals and families at risk?

Attitudes and Identity Development

Cost-benefits and Evaluation of Other Outcomes

- What are the direct costs per prisoner for incarceration, taking into account lost wages, prison construction and staffing, etc.? What cost savings can be realized from the implementation of effective programs prior to, during, and after incarceration?
- What interventions have the most promising long-term outcomes?
- Does the duration of incarceration impact outcomes? Does the uncertainty of prison release timing impact how well prison administrators and faith- and community-based organizations are able to prepare for release?
- How necessary is "knifing off from the past" to assure positive outcomes? Can faith- and community- based organizations create structures to support the ability of released prisoners to separate from the past and experience identity transformation into "family men"?
- Do interventions evaluated as effective for one population work for others?

- What interventions have the most promising long-term outcomes?
- What aspects of the environment in which they are delivered can be replicated elsewhere?
- Do interventions evaluated as effective for one population work for other population groups?

B. Research Strategies

While many of the questions posed above require targeted and original research initiatives, possible answers to many of these may be found by mining existing datasets and studies from the criminal justice and social science fields. A number of potential research strategies were cited as being useful in this regard, and included the following:

- ***Use existing datasets.*** There are a number of significant datasets that can provide information on those currently incarcerated, as well as assist in making predictions about factors contributing to incarceration. The Bureau of Justice Statistics collects data on the demographics of prisoners, and these data are updated semiannually. The National Longitudinal Study of Youth 1979 has followed thousands of families for more than 20 years; many of these can be traced within the criminal justice system. A more recent NLSY dataset from 1997 can be used for comparison with the 1979 cohort. John Laub also highlighted data from research (the Gluecks' Juvenile Delinquency Study) following boys in the Massachusetts juvenile justice system; though this cohort is now elderly (with data originating in the 1930s and 1940s, and tracking participants to age 70), they provide excellent longitudinal information on factors affecting criminality.

The Department of Justice also is studying prison rape or prison sexual violence. The Prison Rape Elimination Act is funding prevalence studies, both in men's and women's prisons, as well as juvenile facilities and giving prisons and jails money to develop programs that would try and alleviate sexual violence among prisoners.

- ***Build on lessons from the military.*** While military personnel and the incarcerated are two very different population groups, military families do share the experience of understanding the challenges of a parent being separated physically from the family unit for an extended period of time and concerns about reintegration into the family and community after deployment. The military system has been involved in a number of initiatives for families dealing with these transitions that could provide useful lessons for working with families of the incarcerated. For example, the military has been doing work to assist families with easing the transition to deployment and return which could serve as a model for other forms of transition. There has also been a study of battering interventions with military men, comparing outcomes for different types of programs.

- ***Use studies on "Stages of Change" and transformation.*** Literature on personal transformation has identified four distinct stages (precontemplation, contemplation, change, and long-term support), based on the Stages of Change model, necessary for individuals to experience if they are to make significant life changes. While research on what prompts certain individuals to undergo transformation is scarce, there is considerable study of identity theory and formation and people recovering from trauma that can be examined for relevance to the incarcerated population. Likewise, more studies need to be undertaken with participants in faith-based prison programs, who often exhibit personal transformation, and how these programs have assisted with this process.

- ***Incorporate studies on battered women and child maltreatment.*** Likewise, there are numerous national surveys looking at battering and child abuse. Studies suggested at the symposium included ones by Jackie Campbell at Johns Hopkins University and Gondolf and Fisher's data predicting batterer recidivism. One participant also cited Jory's Intimate Justice Scale, an instrument that can be used to screen for psychological abuse and physical violence. The DHHS Web site also offers comprehensive information about State domestic violence resources.

- ***Obtain input from target populations themselves.*** Attendees at the symposium noted that one of the most valuable resources is the target population itself. Individuals and families should be included in the development and modification of marriage education and family-strengthening curricula to determine what is most relevant to them. The perspective of the family members and former prisoners on issues of marriage and family life must be understood and integrated into programs.

In: Marriage and Incarceration
Editors: Leana H. Venten
ISBN: 978-1-60692-938-4

Chapter 5

MOVING FORWARD

Brandy Bauer, Jamie Hart, Anne Hopewell and Naomi Tein
U.S. Department of Health and Human Services
Office of the Assistant Secretary for Planning and Evaluation

While the purpose of this symposium was not to come to consensus on any of the discussion points, nevertheless there were several areas in which the participants indicated a strong degree of momentum is needed to move forward and learn more about marriage-strengthening and responsible fatherhood programs, their long-term successes, and how these can be applied to the incarcerated population. This section summarizes these discussion points.

The development and implementation of marriage education programs for use in the prison setting requires consideration of many key issues

While the message of the benefits of healthy marriages may be simple, making sure that message is received by couples affected by incarcerations is not. As illustrated in Figure 4, there are numerous individual-, family-, community-, and program-level issues that must be considered and incorporated when developing curricula that work. On the individual and family level, much thought needs to occur regarding the individual's core beliefs, how their interpersonal skills impact on their relationships with partners and children, and how to ensure that the curricula provide supportive role models for those in the program. At the broader program and community level, marriage education really must consider the economic, health, and reentry issues that this population faces and must link adequately with other community mechanisms that can reinforce the ideas contained within the curricula.

Refining marriage strengthening programs to be most effective will require a sustained commitment to learning more about these issues and testing integration strategies. Cultural competency must be realized as a critical element of program design.

Individual and Family Level Considerations

- Holistic, culturally appropriate approach
- Readiness to change and timing of intervention
- Addressing individual's core belief system
- Interpersonal competence
- Impact on individuals
- Relationships with partners
- Relationships with children
- Support and involvement of women and families
- Skills around being more supportive
- Conflict resolution
- Role models of happy and healthy marriages
- Peer-to-peer focus

Program and Community Level Considerations

- Reentry into community
- Links with the community- and faith-based organizations
- Addressing racism
- Economic issues and costs
- Health issues
- "Edutainment"
- Messenger is as important as the message
- Teachings related to the equality wheel
- Sincerity and commitment of staff
- Appropriate training of staff in models
- Evaluation and research to include demonstration of adapting promising practices

Figure 4. Key Issues for Consideration in Marriage Education Curricula.

How Interventions Are Delivered Is Critical to Their Success

It became clear during the discussion that many challenges with the delivery of interventions can impede the likelihood of their success. Wherever possible, programs need to work with existing resources embedded within the criminal justice system to reinforce positive messages. For those prisoners with multiple risks or vulnerabilities, this means that one program alone may not be able to prevent recidivism; instead bundled services – like those based on level of service inventory assessments – that aim to reach offenders at every stage of incarceration may be key to addressing multiple problems.

Continue Conducting Research to Assess What Interventions Work – and Why

What we know about the effectiveness of current programming and interventions for those that are coming out of prisons is very little, and what we need to know is staggering. How specific programs do or do not achieve their goals, the intersections of race, health problems, domestic violence, and other factors are difficult to tease out of the current research on and evaluations of these interventions. Targeted studies of these factors and how they affect decision-making individually and collectively are needed.

Long-Term Follow-Up and Evaluation Should Be Critical Goals

As mentioned previously, the Healthy Marriage Initiative and SVORI and other reentry initiatives are still in their infancy. It is essential that grantees include evaluation of their initiatives into program design and that other independent examinations of long-term outcomes be funded. Marriage and other social supports should be part of any criminal Justice interventions, and individuals with criminal justice involvement and their partners should be examined as a special subpopulation when evaluating marriage education interventions.

References

Baer, D., et al. (January 2006). *Understanding the challenges of prisoner reentry: Research findings from the Urban Institute's Prisoner Reentry Portfolio. Reentry Research Findings.* Washington: Urban Institute Justice Policy Center.

Bureau of Justice Statistics. (2006, September 6). *Study finds more than half of all prison and jail inmates have mental health problems.* Press Release. Washington: Department of Justice.

Cadora, E., Swartz, C. & Gordon, M. (2003). Criminal justice and health and human services: An exploration of overlapping needs, resources, and interests in Brooklyn neighborhoods. In J. Travis, & M. Waul (Eds.), *Prisoners once removed.* Washington: Urban Institute Press.

Centers for Disease Control and Prevention. (2006, April 21). HIV transmission among male inmates in a State prison system – Georgia 1992-2005. *MMWR*, 55(15), 421-426.

Dunford, F. W., et al. (1990). The role of arrest in domestic assault cases: The Omaha police experiment. *Criminology*, *28*, 183.

Finney-Hairston, C. (2001). *Prisoners and families: Parenting issues during incarceration.* Commissioned paper for the Department of Health and Human Services. Retrieved February 16, 2007, from ASPE Web site: http://aspe.hhs.gov/HSP/prison2home02/Hairston.htm.

Fishman, L. (1990). *Women at the wall: A study of prisoners' wives doing time on the outside.* Albany: State University of New York Press.

Gondolf, E. W. & Fisher, E. (1988). *Battered women as survivors: An alternative to treating learned helplessness.* New York: Lexington Books.

Haney, C. (2001). *The psychological impact of incarceration: Implications for post- prison adjustment.* Commissioned paper for the Department of Health and Human Services. Retrieved February 16, 2007, from ASPE Web site: http://aspe.hhs.gov/HSP/prison2home02/Haney.htm

Haney, C. (2005, December). *Reforming punishment: Psychological limits to the pain of imprisonment.* Washington: American Psychological Association Books.

Harrison, P. & Beck, A. J. (2005, October). Prisoners in 2004. *Bureau of Justice Statistics Bulletin.* Washington: Department of Justice.

Johnson, M. P. (November 2000). *Conflict and control: Gender symmetry and asymmetry in domestic violence.* Revision of a paper prepared for the National Institute of Justice Gender Symmetry Workshop, Arlington, VA.

Jory, B. (2004). The intimate justice scale: An instrument to screen for psychological abuse and physical violence in clinical practice. *Journal of Marital and Family Therapy, 30,* 29-44.

Laub, J. & Sampson, R. (2003). *Shared beginnings, divergent lives: Delinquent boys to age 70.* Cambridge, MA: Harvard University Press.

Mumola, C. (August 2000). *Incarcerated parents and their children.* Bureau of Justice Statistics Special Report. Washington: Department of Justice.

Personal Responsibility and Work Opportunity Reconciliation Act of 1996, Section 101 of Public Law, 104-193.

Sampson, R. & Laub, J. (1993). A life-course theory of cumulative disadvantage and the stability of delinquency. In T. P. Thornberry (Ed.), *Developmental theories of crime and delinquency.* New Brunswick, NJ: Transaction Publishers.

WEB RESOURCES

Department of Health and Human Services

ACF Healthy Marriage Initiative
http://www.acf.hhs.gov/healthymarriage/
African American Healthy Marriage Initiative
http://www.acf.hhs.gov/healthymarriage/aa_hmi/AAHMI.html

Family Violence Prevention and Services Program
http://www.acf.hhs.gov/programs/fysb/content/familyviolence/index.htm

Responsible Fatherhood Initiative
http://fatherhood.hhs.gov

Hispanic Health Marriage Initiative
http://www.acf.hhs.gov/healthymarriage/about/hispanic_hm_initiative.html

Mentoring Children of Prisoners (MCP) Program
http://www.acf.hhs.gov/programs/fysb/content/youthdivision/mcp/index.htm

National Healthy Marriage Resource Center
http://www.healthymarriageinfo.org/

Native American Healthy Marriage Initiative
http://www.acf.hhs.gov/programs/ana/programs/NAHMI.html

Department of Justice

Bureau of Justice Statistics, Department of Justice
www.ojp.usdoj.gov/bjs/

DOJ Office on Violence Against Women
http://www.usdoj.gov/ovw/

Multisite Evaluation of the Serious and Violent Offender Reentry Initiative (SVORI)
http://www.svori-evaluation.org/

Serious and Violent Offender Reentry Initiative (SVORI)
http://www.reentry.gov/

Other

Department of Labor Center for Faith-Based and Community Initiatives
http://www.dol.gov/cfbci/Ready4Work.htm

Institute on Domestic Violence in the African American Community
http://www.dvinstitute.org/

President's Re-entry Initiative (PRI)
http://www.doleta.gov/pri/

Vera Institute of Justice, Safe Return Initiative
http://www.vera.org/project/project1_1.asp?section_id=8&project_id=27

White House Office of Faith-Based and Community Initiatives
http://www.whitehouse.gov/government/fbci/

In: Marriage and Incarceration
Editors: Leana H. Venten
ISBN: 978-1-60692-938-4

Appendix A

SYMPOSIUM AGENDA

RESEARCH AND PRACTICE SYMPOSIUM ON MARRIAGE AND INCARCERATION

L 'Enfant Plaza Hotel Washington, DC
April 20–21, 2006

Purpose of the Symposium: The purpose of this symposium is to understand more fully the strategies for improving outcomes for couples who want to develop healthy marriages during and after one partner's incarceration. By convening a diverse group of experts with research and practice knowledge about incarceration and reentry, marriage strengthening, family processes, and domestic violence, this symposium will begin to identify research and program development needs that could be addressed by public- and/or private-sector investment in research and practice. Based on facilitated discussion on a variety of topics, the symposium participants will develop a framework for next steps in expanding marriage strengthening education services and research for couples separated by incarceration.

The outcomes anticipated from the meeting include:

- Increase in understanding among the criminal justice and marriage education disciplines about how this issue is viewed from the other side's perspective

- Identification of practice needs and gaps in order to improve marriage outcomes for these couples
- Review of research topics for improved understanding of the efficacy of various interventions for this population.

Thursday, April 20

10:00 a.m. **Introductions and Opening Remarks**

- Jamie Hart, Facilitator, Health System's Research. Inc.
- Jerry Regier, Deputy Assistant Secretary, Human Services Policy

11:00 a.m. **Session 1: Framing Remarks and Facilitated Discussion**

What are the social, psychological, and environmental circumstances of incarceration (and reentry) that are likely to affect marriage and family functioning?

- Creasie Finney Hairston, University of Illinois–Chicago
- Craig Haney, University of California–Santa Cruz

12:00–1:00 p.m. **Working Lunch**

- Participants will have an opportunity to learn from their colleagues about their research and practice experience.

1:00–2:45 p.m. **Session 1: Facilitated Discussion (continued)**

2:45–3:00 p.m. **Break**

3:00–4:50 p.m. **Session 2: Framing Remarks and Facilitated Discussion**

How do marriage-strengthening curricula and edu-cational programming address the specific vulnera-bilities of couples affected by incarceration and release?

- Howard Markman, University of Denver
- Lorraine Blackman, Indiana University School of Social Work

4:50–5:00 p.m. **Closing – Overview of Day 2**

Friday, April 21

8:00 a.m. **Continental Breakfast**

8:30–10:15 a.m. **Session 3: Framing Remarks and Facilitated Discussion**

There are critical concerns raised by the high potential for domestic violence in this population. What are the known strategies and skills that could reduce the risk of possible harm to partners and children?

- Amy Holtzworth-Munroe, Indiana University–Bloomington
- Oliver Williams, University of Minnesota and Institute on Domestic Violence in the African American Community

10:30 a.m.–12:00 p.m. **Session 4: Facilitated Discussion**

What should to be added to marriage curricula in order to better address the social, psychological, and environmental circumstances of incarceration (and reentry) and the potential for domestic violence?

What community support mechanisms are important to increase the chances of marital stability and success for this population?

12:00–1:00 p.m. **Working Lunch**

- Begin discussion on research and practice needs

1:00–2:45 p.m. **Session 5: Framing Remarks and Facilitated Discussion**

What additional research and practice knowledge do we need to more forward in developing marriage education programs for this population?

- Randy Day, Brigham Young University
- Robert Lerman, Urban Institute and American University

2:45–3:00 p.m. **Closing Remarks**

- Jerry Regier, Deputy Assistant Secretary, HSP

In: Marriage and Incarceration
Editors: Leana H. Venten
ISBN: 978-1-60692-938-4

Appendix B

PARTICIPANTS AT THE SYMPOSIUM

RESEARCH AND PRACTICE SYMPOSIUM ON MARRIAGE AND INCARCERATION

L 'Enfant Plaza Hotel Washington, DC
April 20-21, 2006

Christophe Beard
Associate Director of Corrections Programming
National Fatherhood Initiative
101 Lake Forest Boulevard, Suite 360
Gaithersburg, MD 20877
Phone: 301-948-0599
Fax: 301-948-4325
E-mail: cbeard@fatherhood.org

Marlene Beckman, J.D.
Acting Chief, Justice Systems
National Institute of Justice
Justice Systems Research Division
U.S. Department of Justice
810 Seventh Street, N.W., Fourth Floor
Washington, DC 20530
Phone: 202-616-3562
E-mail: marlene.beckman@usdoj.gov

Lorraine Blackman, Ph.D.
Associate Professor
School of Social Work Indiana University
Education/Social Work Building
ES 4121
902 West New York Street
Indianapolis, IN 46202-5 156
Phone: 317-274-6713
Fax: 317-291-4523
E-mail: lblackma@iupui.edu

Col. Glen Bloomstrom, M.Div., M.S., M.S.S.
Chaplain
Director
Ministry Initiatives Directorate
U.S. Army Chief of Chaplains
1421 Jefferson Davis Highway, Suite 10600
Arlington, VA 22202-3259
Phone: 703-601-0074
Fax: 703-601-4455
E-mail: glen.l.bloomstrom@us.army.mil

Jason Bohn
Emerging Leader
U.S. Department of Health and Human Services
200 Independence Avenue, S.W., Room 404E12
Washington, DC 20201
Phone: 202-690-7927
E-mail: jason.bohn@hhs.gov

Jennifer Burnszynski
Social Science Analyst
Human Services Policy
Office of the Assistant Secretary for Planning and Evaluation
U.S. Department of Health and Human Services
200 Independence Avenue, S.W., Room 404E
Washington, DC 20201
Phone: 202-690-8651
Fax: 202-690-6562

E-mail: jennifer.burnszynski@hhs.gov

Anne Brown
Director of Planning
Offender Services
Department of Corrections
420 Watson Powell Jr. Way
Des Moines, IA 50309
Phone: 515-242-5729
Fax: 515-281-7345
E-mail: anne.brown@iowa.gov

Natasha Cabrera, Ph.D., M.A.
Assistant Professor
College of Education
Human Development
University of Maryland
3304 North Benjamin Building, Room 3 304N
College Park, MD 20742
Phone: 301-405-2801
Fax: 301-405-2891
E-mail: ncabrera@umd.edu

Nancye Campbell
Research Analyst
Office of Planning, Research and Evaluation
Administration for Children and Families
U.S. Department of Health and Human Services
Aerospace Building, Seventh Floor
370 L'Enfant Plaza, S.W.
Washington, DC 20447
Phone: 202-401-5760
Fax: 202-205-3598
E-mail: ncampbell@acf.hhs.gov

Bill Coffin, M.Ed.
Special Assistant for Marriage Education
Office of the Assistant Secretary
Administration for Children and Families

U.S. Department of Health and Human Services
901 D Street, S.W., Suite 600W
Washington, DC 20447
Phone: 202-260-1550
Fax: 202-401-5770
E-mail: bcoffin@acf.hhs.gov

Diann Dawson
Director
Office of Regional Operations
Administration for Children and Families
U.S. Department of Health and Human Services
Aerospace Building, Sixth Floor
370 L'Enfant Plaza, S.W.
Washington, DC 20447
Phone: 202-401-9277
Fax: 202-401-5776
E-mail: ddawson@acf.hhs.gov

Randal Day, Ph.D.
Professor of Family Life
School of Family Life
Brigham Young University
Room 2092B
1041 JFSB
Provo, UT 84602-67 10
Phone: 801-422-6415
Fax: 801-422-0225
E-mail: day@byu.edu

Hazel D. Dean, Sc.D., M.P.H.
Associate Director for Health Disparities
National Center for HIV, STD, and TB Prevention
Coordinating Center for Infectious Diseases
Centers for Disease Control and Prevention
1600 Clifton Road, N.E., MSE-07 Atlanta, GA 30333
Phone: 404-639-8009
Fax: 404-639-8629
E-mail: hdean@cdc.gov

Allison Deschamps, Ph.D.
SRCD Policy Fellow
Office of Planning, Research and Evaluation
Administration for Children and Families
U.S. Department of Health and Human Services
370 L'Enfant Plaza, S.W.
Washington, DC 20447
Phone: 202-205-8115
E-mail: adeschamps@acf.hhs.gov

JoAnne Eason, B.B.A.
Vice-President
Oklahoma Marriage Institute
Public Strategies
301 Northwest 63rd Street, Suite 600
Oklahoma City, OK 73116
Phone: 405-848-2171
Fax: 405-848-2078
E-mail: joanne.eason@publicstrategies.com

Jeff Evans, Ph.D., J.D.
Director of Intergenerational Research
Demographic and Behavioral Sciences Branch
National Institute of Child Health and Human Services
National Institute of Health
6100 Executive Boulevard, Room 8B07
Bethesda, MD 21012
Phone: 301-496-1176
Fax: 301-496-0962
E-mail: jeff_evans@nih.gov

David Fein
Senior Associate
Social and Economic Policy Division
Abt Associates, Inc.
4550 Montgomery Avenue, Suite 800
Bethesda, MD 20814
Phone: 301-634-1851
Fax: 301-634-1703
E-mail: david_fein@abtassociates.com

Mark Fucello
Social Science Analyst
Office of Planning, Research and Evaluation
Administration for Children and Families
U.S. Department of Health and Human Services
Aerospace Building, Seventh Floor
370 L'Enfant Plaza, S.W.
Washington, DC 20447
Phone: 202-401-5750
E-mail: mfucello@acf.hhs.gov

Frank Fuentes
(Represented by Suelle Diaz)
Deputy Commisioner
Administration on Children, Youth and Families
Administration for Children and Families
U.S. Department of Health and Human Services
1250 Maryland Avenue, S.W., Eighth Floor
Washington, DC 20024
Phone: 202-401-2910
Fax: 202-260-9336
E-mail: ffuentes@acf.hhs.gov

John Graff, B.A., M.A., J.D.
Prison Fellowship Minstries
8356 Queen Elizabeth Boulevard
Annadale, VA 22003
Phone: 703-425-5276
Fax: 703-425-0432
E-mail: jgraff1@cox.net

Creasie Finney Hairston, Ph.D.
Dean, Professor of Social Work
Jane Addam's College of Social Work
University of Illinois, Chicago
MC 309, Room 4010, ECSW
1040 West Harrison
Chicago, IL 60607-7134
Phone: 312-996-3219
Fax: 312-996-1802

E-mail: cfh@uic.edu

Craig Haney, Ph.D.
Professor
Department of Psychology
University of California
115 Social Sciences 2
Santa Cruz, CA 95064
Phone: 831-459-2153
E-mail: psylaw@ucsc.edu

Ron Haskins
Senior Fellow
Center on Children and Families
Economic Studies Program
The Brookings Institution
1775 Massachusetts Avenue, N.W.
Washington, DC 20036-2188
Phone: 202-797-6057
E-mail: rhaskins@brookings.edu

Robert Hendricks
Policy Advisor
Office of Justice Programs
Bureau of Justice Assistance
U.S. Department of Justice
810 Seventh Street, N.W.
Washington, DC 20531
Phone: 202-305-1909
E-mail: robert.hendricks@usdoj.gov

Gina R. Hijjawi, Ph.D.
AAAS/SRCD Executive Branch Fellow
National Institute on Drug Abuse
Prevention Research Branch
Division of Epidemiology, Services, and
Prevention Research
6001 Executive Boulevard
Room 5185, MSC 9589

Bethesda, MD 20892-9589.
Phone: 301-594-4381
Fax: 301-480-2542
E-mail: hijjawig@nida.nih.gov

Amy Holtzworth-Munroe, Ph.D.
Professor of Psychology
College of Arts and Sciences
Department of Psychology
Indiana University
1101 East 10th Street
Bloomington, IN 47405-7007
Phone: 812-855-8159
Fax: 812-855-4691
E-mail: holtzwor@indiana.edu

Pamela Jordan, Ph.D., R.N.
Associate Professor
Department of Family and Child Nursing
University of Washington
Box 357262
Seattle, WA 98195-7262
Phone: 206-427-7848
Fax: 206-543-6656
E-mail: pjordan@u.washington.edu

Pamela Lattimore, Ph.D.
Professor
Department of Criminology and Criminal Justice
University of South Carolina Senior Research Social Scientist
Center for Crime, Violence, and Justice Research
Research Triangle Institute 3040 Cornwallis Drive
Research Triangle Park, NC 27709
212 Winding Oak Way
Blythewood, SC 29016
Phone: 803-754-5965
Fax: 919-485-7700
E-mail: lattimore@rti.org

John Laub, Ph.D.
Professor
Department of Criminology and Criminal Justice
University of Maryland
2220 LeFrak Hall
College Park, MD 20742-8235
Phone: 301-405-8070
Fax: 301-405-4733
E-mail: jlaub@crim.umd.edu

Robert Lerman, Ph.D.
Professor, American University
Senior Fellow
Urban Institute, LHP
2100 M Street, N.W., Room 5183
Washington, DC 20037
Phone: 202-261-5676
Fax: 202-463-8522
E-mail: blerman@ui.urban.org

Howard Markman, Ph.D.
Professor and Co-Director
Center for Marital and Family Studies
Department of Psychology
University of Denver
Frontier Hall, Room 212
2155 South Race Street
Denver, CO 80208
Phone: 303-871-3370
Fax: 303-871-4747
E-mail: hmarkman@du.edu

Sheena McConnell
Associate Director and Senior Economist
Mathematica Policy Research
600 Maryland Avenue, S.W.
Washington, DC 20024
Phone: 202-484-4518
E-mail: smcconnell@mathematica-mpr.com

Linda Mellgren
Senior Social Science Analyst
Human Services Policy
Office of the Assistant Secretary for Planning and Evaluation
U.S. Department of Health and Human Services
200 Independence Avenue, S.W.
Washington, DC 20201
Phone: 202-690-6806
E-mail: linda.mellgren@hhs.gov

Anne Menard, B.A.
Director
National Resource Center on Domestic Violence
6400 Flank Drive, Suite 1300
Harrisburg, PA 17112
Phone: 800-537-2238
Fax: 717-545-6400
E-mail: amenard@pcadv.org

Charles Michalopoulos
Senior Fellow
MDRC
16 East 34th Street
New York, NY 10016-4326
Phone: 212-340-8692
Fax: 212-684-0832
E-mail: michalo@mdrc.org

Cheri Nolan
Senior Advisor to the Administrator
Substance Abuse and Mental Health Services Administration
U.S. Department of Health and Human Services
One Choke Cherry Road
Room 8-1057
Rockville, MD 20852
Phone: 240-276-2005
E-mail: cheri.nolan@samsha.hhs.gov

Jerry Regier
Deputy Assistant Secretary
Human Services Policy
Office of the Assistant Secretary for Planning and Evaluation
U.S. Department of Health and Human Services
200 Independence Avenue, S.W.
Washington, DC 20201
Phone: 202-690-7409
E-mail: jerry.regier@hhs.gov

William Alvarado Rivera, J.D.
Acting Deputy Commissioner
Office of Child Support Enforcement
Administation for Children and Families
U.S. Department of Health and Human Services
370 L'Enfant Plaza, S.W.
Washington, DC 20447
Phone: 202-401-9370
Fax: 202-401-5655
E-mail: wrivera@acf.hhs.gov

David H. Siegel
Deputy Associate Commissioner
Family and Youth Services Bureau
Administration for Children and Families
U.S. Department of Health and Human Services
1250 Maryland Avenue, S.W.
Washington, DC 20024
Phone: 202-205-8102
Fax: 202-401-5533
E-mail: dsiegel@acf.hhs.gov

Sarah Skriloff
Healthy Marriage Program Specialist
Administation for Native Americans
U.S. Department of Health and Human Services
370 L'Enfant Promenade, S.W.
Washington, DC 20447
Phone: 202-205-4328

Fax: 202-690-7441
E-mail: sskriloff@acf.hhs.gov

Greg Weltz
Director
Division of Youth Services
Office of Workforce Investments/ Employment and Training Administration
U.S. Department of Labor
200 Constitution Avenue, N.W., Room N4459
Washington, DC 20210
Phone: 202-693-3030
Fax: 202-693-3861
E-mail: weltz.greg@dol.gov

Oliver Williams
Professor
University of Minnestoa School of Social Work
Executive Director
Institute on Domestic Violence in the African American Community
105 Peters Hall
1404 Gortner Avenue
St. Paul, MN 55108
Phone: 612-624-9217
E-mail: owilliam@umn.edu

HSR Staff

Jamie Hart, Ph.D., M.P.H.
Director, Intercultural Health Practice Area
Health Systems Research, Inc.
1200 1 8th Street, N.W., Suite 700
Washington, DC 20036
Phone: 202-828-5100
Fax: 202-728-9469
E-mail: jhart@hsrnet.com

Anne Hopewell, M.S.W.
Senior Associate
Health Systems Research, Inc.
1200 1 8th Street, N.W., Suite 700
Washington, DC 20036
Phone: 202-828-5100
Fax: 202-728-9469
E-mail: ahopewell@hsrnet.com

Joy King
Senior Meetings Manager
Health Systems Research, Inc.
1200 1 8th Street, N.W., Suite 700
Washington, DC 20036
Phone: 202-828-5100
Fax: 202-728-9469
E-mail: jking@hsrnet.com

Naomi Tein
Senior Policy Associate
Health Systems Research, Inc.
1200 1 8th Street, N.W., Suite 700
Washington, DC 20036
Phone: 202-828-5100
Fax: 202-728-9469
E-mail: ntein@hsrnet.com

In: Marriage and Incarceration
Editors: Leana H. Venten
ISBN: 978-1-60692-938-4

Appendix C

FROM PRISON TO HOME RESOURCE PAPER

A. BACKGROUND OF THE FROM PRISON TO HOME PROJECT

In 2002, the DHHS brought together a range of stakeholders from the criminal justice and health and human services research and practice communities to discuss how children and families are affected by the incarceration of a parent. That planning for that conference, *The Effects of Incarceration and Reentry on Children, Families and Communities*, was predicated upon the recognition of two facts: first, that there has been

a significant in the number of imprisoned individuals in the United States and a concomitant increase in the number of children and families affected by parental incarceration; second, that while there has been an increasing body of work in the area of incarceration and prisoner reentry, it was difficult to find programs and policies focusing specifically on facilitating the incarceration and reentry process for families and children.

As part of the planning for the *From Prison to Home* conference, ASPE collaborated with the Urban Institute to commission a series of working papers aimed at developing a research and practice baseline for this high-risk, high-services use population. These papers served as the touchstone for the discussions at the invitation-only conference held in January 2002. The DHHS also convened a State Symposium prior to the conference to discuss with state policy makers in Maryland, Nevada, Oregon, Pennsylvania, and Wisconsin barriers and opportunities for implementing cross-cutting strategies involving criminal justice and health and human services systems. Subsequently, HSR was awarded a contract from ASPE to continue work on the *From Prison to Home* issue through two means: (1) by providing logistical and facilitation support to groups of experts to discuss these issues further and (2) by producing a synthesis of the research and practice issues that would be identified in such future meetings. The *Research and Practice Symposium on Marriage and Incarceration* is part of that effort.

If there is a common theme to the papers presented at the *From Prison to Home* 2002 conference, it is the need for further research in multiple disciplines related to the children, families, and communities impacted by incarceration. Each of the papers suggested a variety of research questions involving disciplines beyond corrections and justice, including family systems theory, child development, sociology, gender studies, and economics to name just a few. Despite worthy evaluation efforts devoted to a wide range of rehabilitative interventions, these larger research issues have not yet attracted sufficient attention from researchers, scholars, and funders. Yet the families and communities impacted by incarceration share many commonalties with other families who suffer from poverty, dislocation, and trauma. Joining these different research strands not only will inform future strategies for preventing or rehabilitating individuals involved with the criminal justice system, but also will enrich the knowledge base to serve all families and communities struggling for family stability and financial self-sufficiency.

What follows is a brief synopsis of the complex themes that emerged from each on the paper written for the conference, followed by questions that can be used to guide further research on how incarceration impacts child development, family processes, and community functioning. This is not intended to represent a synthesis of all the current research in the field, but to convey the specific research gaps and needs identified by each of the paper's authors. And indeed, there has been a significant increase in attention to these issues since 2002. However, it is anticipated that this information can aid in the discussion of the research and practice knowledge that is needed to understand better the children, families, and communities impacted by incarceration.

B. Summary of the Research Papers and Questions

Papers on Children Affected by Incarceration

Despite a significant number of studies having been conducted around individuals affected by incarceration, very little research to date has been devoted specifically to examining incarceration's effects on children. The *From Prison to Home* researchers noted that further study is needed at all stages of a child's development, from being present at a parent's arrest to the long-term outcomes and adult behavioral patterns of children of ex-offenders.

- ***Stephanie Covington, A Woman's Journey Home: Challenges for Female Offenders and Their Children.*** Covington discusses the intersection of substance abuse and mental health with incarceration but focuses specifically on how these issues impact women and their relationships with their children. She cites the invisibility of women in the criminal justice system and the need to reassess the level of burden imposed by trauma and substance abuse on women, and how these affect noncompliance with treatment. She also highlights some gender-responsive models of success, such as The Refugee Model and Our Place in Washington, DC, that attempt to deal with trauma in women's lives as one of the root causes of criminality. Covington asserts that gender considerations require a reworking of the current corrections system to incorporate the relational needs specific to women.

- ***J. Mark Eddy and John B. Reid, The Antisocial Behavior of the Adolescent Children of Incarcerated Parents: A Developmental Perspective.*** This paper discusses the possible links between parent criminality and adolescent child antisocial behavior, including the yet unproven link between incarceration and such behavior. The authors suggest that it is critical to study the context of family relationships and functioning to determine what factors promote resiliency and mitigate negative outcomes in the face of parental criminality. Eddy and Reid also call for further examination of parenting programs within the prison setting, and other interventions, to ascertain whether they can and do make a difference in adolescents' lives.

- ***Ross Parke and K. Alison Clarke-Stewart. Effects of Parental Incarceration on Young Children.*** Parke and Clarke-Stewart's paper emphasizes the need for additional study on the short- and long-term effects of a child having an imprisoned parent, and the need to understand more about these families using a variety of psychological frameworks. This paper specifically examines prison programming that has the goal of enhancing an inmate's ability to provide a supportive, nurturing environment for their children upon release. These studies investigate classes, workshops and interventions that teach inmates appropriate post-release life skills to help their children cope with the stresses of having an incarcerated parent. Parke and Clarke-Stewart also stress the need for longitudinal studies that pay particular attention to gender, culture, ethnicity, and family processes.

Research Questions on Child Development Issues

Parent-child Relationships:

- What impact does the quality of the preprison parent-child relationship have on how well children fare following separation from the parent due to incarceration?
- Is there an identifiable relationship between the nature of the parent's crime, and the quality of the parent-child relationship during and after incarceration?
- What psychological effects are seen in children who shift caregivers due to long-term incarceration or release of a parent? Do these effects differ depending on the gender of the incarcerated parent? How do they compare to children separated from their parents by the foster care system or divorce?
- How does a parent's mental illness or substance abuse impact the parent-child relationship prior to, during, and after incarceration?
- What are the developmental impacts of exposure to the prison environment (e.g., through visitation) on the parent-child relationship?
- What are the short- and long-term psychological impacts on a child who witnesses a parent's arrest?
- Do particular aspects of the early parent-child relationship predispose children to engage in antisocial behavior in adolescence?

Living Arrangements and Separation:

- In what ways does the impact of parent-child separation due to incarceration differ when compared to divorce and death?
- In what ways are the psychological impacts of incarceration on children who do not live with their parent prior to incarceration different than the psychological impacts on those who do?

Resiliency and Delinquency:

- How does the gender of the incarcerated parent correlate to the likelihood of their children exhibiting delinquency, antisocial, and other discordant behavior?
- Is there a relationship between parental incarceration and adolescent antisocial behavior? If so, what associations can be made between the age of a child at the time of a parent's arrest and subsequent adolescent antisocial behavior?
- What are the factors that increase resiliency in children of incarcerated parents and are the developmental outcomes different if these factors are in place prior to, during, or after the incarceration?
- How do substance use or mental health disorders impact the resiliency of both parents and children following incarceration?

Papers on Families

The gaps in our knowledge about the effects of incarceration on children include a lack of information about its long-term effects on family functioning. The authors of these papers called for further research into factors such as race, caregiving, family configuration, and skills and deficits of parents, and how these contribute to or impede families being able to transcend the negative outcomes associated with incarceration.

- ***Gerald Gaes and Newton Kendig, The Skills Sets and Health Care Needs of Released Offenders.*** The primary foci of Gaes and Kendig's work emphasize the necessity of developing a needs assessment for prisoners to determine what programming is most beneficial to them and their families, and then assessing how many prisoners receive these services. The authors present a detailed skills matrix which outlines the basic abilities needed for offenders to lead productive lives both within and outside of the corrections environment, including such academic skills as reading and computation, and learned behaviors such as parenting and family budgeting. Gaes and Kendig also suggest conducting cost-benefit analyses to determine the potential financial gains achieved when prisoners who receive programming are able to return to their families successfully.

- ***Creasie Finney Hairston, Prisoners and Families: Parenting Issues During Incarceration.*** Highlighting the various problems encountered on a family level as a result of incarceration, Hairston's work posits the need for a more flexible definition of family, and focuses on the presence of family ties that may mitigate risk, enhance resiliency, and improve outcomes. She calls for additional research into how financial distress, race, and gender of the offender parent, as well as differing caregiver arrangements for children, affect family outcomes. Hairston also notes preliminary evidence that welfare reform legislation that was intended to keep children in stable homes may have negatively impacted the ability of offenders to retain custody of their children. There is little understanding, however, of what happens to these children developmentally as well as what impact these changes in child custody has on overall child welfare and the court system that serves these families.

Research Questions Regarding Family Process Issues

Family Arrangements and Relationships:

- What are the characteristics of families whose children exhibit successful outcomes yet live in difficult contexts (e.g., poverty, frequent home or school transition, incarceration)?
- In what ways does the nature of the family configuration (married couple, extended kin network, etc.) prior to incarceration impact the experience of incarceration and the reentry process?
- What is the impact of incarceration on those caregivers that take on a "gatekeeper" role in maintaining the parent-child relationship during separation? Is there a difference in this impact depending on whether this caregiver is another parent, family member, or non-relative?
- What are the impacts of increased periods of separation (or non-visitation) on the parent-child dyad, the extended family, and the offenders' mothers and their subsequent interactions with their grandchildren?
- In what ways does incarceration impact the relationship between married couples? Between couples who are cohabitating? Between couples who are neither married nor live together yet share responsibility or custody of

children? How can the current understanding on marital communication skills and challenges be used to support these couples?

- How does incarceration impact on a parent's ability to coparent a child?
- How is relational theory – which emphasizes the situatedness (historically, culturally, and socially) of human behavior and experience – associated with the type of crime and incarceration experience of both male and female offenders?
- How do the unique social roles of males and females affect their ability to transcend the negative consequences of incarceration?
- How do the corrections and rehabilitation environments impact men's and women's parenting roles?

Parenting:

- What behaviors of incarcerated parents serve to alleviate or exacerbate stressors on children?
- How can incarcerated parents play a non-negative role in their children's lives?
- How does the age at which people become parents and the length of time of their relationship with their children affect their ability to transcend negative consequences of incarceration?

Postprison Impact:

- How does the prison environment impact familial relationships, both during incarceration and following the return of prisoners to their communities?
- How is a family impacted by reunion with released family members?
- What are the impacts of multiple family members entering and exiting prison on the reunion and reentry experience for those families? Does this experience differ from families of military, Seasonal Migrant, or other transitioning households?

Papers on Communities

Several of the papers, while examining what is and is not known about incarceration's effects on children and families, also discussed what effects cycles of incarceration may be having on communities and the functioning of neighborhoods. These papers explored recidivism at the community level, the prison environment, and how programming within and outside of the prison setting may contribute to community instability and negative outcomes for reentering offenders.

- ***James Austin, John Irwin, and Patricia Hardyman, Exploring the Needs and Risks of the Returning Prisoner Population.*** Austin et al. address the issue of recidivism and attempt to analyze it at the community level, using sample studies from communities in three States – Kentucky, Pennsylvania, and Texas. They note that gender, age, residential stability, and employment all factor into rates of recidivism. The authors also posit that changes in sentencing policy over the past two decades has only intensified prison's debilitating effects on families and communities. They cite the need to understand more about how recidivism is affected by social stress and disorganization in communities, the rise in number of female (especially parents) offenders, and the increase in number of nonviolent offenders serving life terms.

- ***Craig Haney, The Psychological Impact of Incarceration: Implications for Postprison Adjustment.*** Haney's paper focuses on the psychological effects of imprisonment that have been exacerbated by society's increased usage of supermax facilities and solitary confinement. He stresses the impacts these have on mental health not only of healthy prisoners, but also on special populations, such as the roughly 20 percent of offenders with existing mental or developmental disorders. Haney hypothesizes that facilities like this have negative implications for those transitioning to home and offer little opportunity for prisoners to acquire autonomy that can help them adapt to post-prison life. He also discusses how the movement away from the goal of rehabilitation towards practices such as mandatory sentencing, three strikes policies and the trying of juveniles as adults has changed the prison experience. He questions the long-term viability of these practices both for moral and practical reasons, such as the realities of increased resources needed to house and treat an expanding and aging prison population.

- ***Dina Rose and Todd Clear, Incarceration, Reentry and Social Capital: Social Networks in the Balance.*** Rose and Clear address the issue of how neighborhoods play a part in crime, and discuss the role of social capital and collective efficacy in channeling resources into crime prevention. They also discuss larger issues of financial problems and stigma that result from incarceration and how these strain families of ex-offenders, and cite several promising models for how communities can enhance collective capacity to improve the process of reentry.

- ***Shelli Rossman, Services Integration: Strengthening Offenders and Families, While Promoting Community Health and Safety.*** In her paper, Rossman addresses the fragmentation of service delivery, particularly as it relates to health care for incarcerated and newly released individuals. She discusses how the differing mentalities between corrections versus health providers often mean prisoners with significant physical, mental health and substance abuse problems do not receive appropriate, coordinated treatment. Rossman particularly notes that while we have some data on risk for infectious disease and substance abuse, there is little information on transmission of disease, how often offenders are able to access treatment, and the care they receive upon release. She highlights a number of promising models for how collaboration between corrections and health entities has worked, mostly around HIV-positive offenders, and those with mental illness, and urges for replication and further study of these models in other settings. She also discusses the importance of accessible, integrated health services to meet the physical and mental health needs of individuals upon their release.

Research on community functioning issues

Gender and Race Issues:

- How do sociocultural gender stereotypes impact how communities or the public perceive the incarcerated?
- To what extent does the level of "caring capacity" within a community mitigate or increase the risk for women's incarceration?
- Do the corrections and rehabilitation environments have different impacts on both men's and women's ability to reconnect in the community?
- What are the long term implications for the African-American population, when a high percentage of its men are imprisoned during what should be their most productive years?

Social Capital and Collective Efficacy:

- What associations can be made between the characteristics of a community and the types of crimes committed in its neighborhoods?
- What are the impacts of unemployment and poverty on collective efficacy – that is, "the combination of trust and cohesion with shared expectations for control" – within communities?
- What qualities of individual neighborhoods are associated with having greater or less social organization?
- Do families from higher socioeconomic brackets suffer the same long-term effects as those from less affluent communities?
- What elements and levels of social capital within communities contribute to the successes or failures of children when social capital is defined as "a byproduct of social relationships that provides the capacity for collective understanding and action"?
- What is the association between the number of offenders on probation or parole and the level of social capital and collective efficacy in a given community?
- What is the impact of a parent's release from prison on existing social service delivery practices operating in communities, especially those targeted to families and children?

Reentry Issues:

- What educational and behavioral skills are needed by reentering offenders to enable them to transition successfully and prevent recidivism and how can these skills best be developed and reinforced?
- What implications do health conditions such as mental illness, substance abuse, and infectious disease have for reentry? What are the associations between these conditions and the level of acceptance offered by communities for ex-offenders?
- Is there an association between specific trauma pathways (e.g., child abuse, sexual assault) and the types of crime committed? Or an association between trauma pathways and resiliency and recidivism?
- How does the nature of the prison environment affect the goals, values, and attitudes of the incarcerated and their ability to reenter a community successfully?

C. Drawing Conclusions

The research questions presented above attempt to further elucidate some of the unanswered research questions posed at the *From Prison to Home* conference and begin to posit a framework for future investigation. Since it is clear that this is an underresearched field of study, it is important to consider future research needs that includes the following characteristics: a global perspective, openness to research designs that cross disciplines, and the inclusion of diverse research teams.

A Broad Perspective

In light of the current trend towards punishment and long-term imprisonment, an ever- increasing number of individuals are being involved in the criminal justice system. Despite a predisposition to preclude these individuals from the larger society, they share many characteristics with ordinary parents, workers, or other marginalized populations. Research that overlooks the commonalties between and among all individuals and families is limited in its application to a variety of fields.

In addition, it should be acknowledged that the growing number of families and communities impacted by imprisonment and release do not exist in isolation from the rest of the population. They are part of our workforce, our social service system, and our schools and faith communities. Lessons learned on how to prevent or mitigate criminal behavior only can improve quality of life for all families. Future research should focus not only on those directly affected by incarceration but also on the implications for the United States as a whole. Research currently underway in Europe can spark rich debate on the broader implications of our criminal justice system.

Research That Crosses Disciplines

Many research disciplines are undergoing rapid transformation in the age of information technology. Social science research tools are becoming more sophisticated, data collection methods are improving, and the distribution of important research outcomes is enhanced by the Internet. As more is learned about brain development, trauma, and parenting, this knowledge base should be examined from a criminal justice perspective. Conversely, imprisonment impacts the physical, mental, developmental, and behavioral aspects of a person. By its very nature, future research studies on the children, families, and communities of incarcerated persons must be designed to integrate these various biopsychosocial perspectives.

Diversity of Research Teams

Combining a broad perspective and cross discipline research designs necessitates the development of diverse research teams. In many instances, researchers from different fields will need to develop a common idiom. Care must be taken to create equal partnerships that value the education and experience of all professions. By creating teams from a variety of disciplines, much is gained. In an era of limited financial resources for research projects with narrow application, diverse research teams can involve a number of different funding streams. As the knowledge base of the human and societal costs of incarceration increases, the results can be shared across specialties. This will broaden the application of results beyond just the traditional fields that have studied criminal justice in the past to include professionals who interact with a number of different populations.

The questions posed herein and by the authors of the commissioned papers provide a starting point from which to engage researchers from a range of disciplines to develop widespread, longitudinal studies regarding these issues. It is hoped that through the creation of such efforts, the research findings will improve the lives and functioning of all children, families, and communities.

Chapter Sources

The following chapters have been previously published:

All Chapters are an edited, reformatted and augmented edition of a United States Department of Health and Human Services, Office of the Assistant Secretary for Planning and Evaluation publication, dated January 2007.

INDEX

D

E

F

G

H

I

J

K

L

M

N

O

P

Q

R

S